P9-CMY-620

Simply
Sparkling
CHRISTMAS
BEADING

23
7
3
8
15

Simply Sparkling CHRISTMAS BEADING

Dorothy Wood

A DAVID & CHARLES BOOK

David & Charles is an F+W Publications Inc. company
4700 East Galbraith Road
Cincinnati, OH 45236

First published in the UK in 2007

A catalogue record for this book is available from the British Library.

ISBN-13: 978-0-7153-2593-3 hardback
ISBN-10: 0-7153-2593-0 hardback

ISBN-13: 978-0-7153-2543-8 paperback
ISBN-10: 0-7153-2543-4 paperback

Printed in China by SNP Leefung
for David & Charles
Brunel House Newton Abbot Devon

Executive Editor Cheryl Brown
Desk Editor Bethany Dymond
Project Editor Lin Clements
Head of Design Prudence Rogers
Production Controller Ros Napper
Photographer Simon Whitmore

Visit our website at www.davidandcharles.co.uk

David & Charles books are available from all good bookshops; alternatively you
can contact our Orderline on 0870 9908222 or write to us at FREEPOST EX2 110,
D&C Direct, Newton Abbot, TQ12 4ZZ (no stamp required UK only); US customers
call 800-289-0963 and Canadian customers call 800-840-5220.

Contents

Introduction

The weeks leading up to Christmas are exciting and busy as there are so many things to get ready. With the home to decorate, gifts to organize and cards to send, it's a surprise that any of us have the energy left to enjoy the big day itself!

It is also an inspiring time because the shops are filled with so many gorgeous things and the displays are so wonderful. It is tempting simply to buy everything you need, but where's the fun in that? It's much more stimulating to be inspired by the colours and styles that you've seen and make your own festive creations. Friends and family will just love a handmade gift or card and visitors to your home will adore the beautiful decorations that you have made.

Christmas has long been a time full of sparkle and glitter and there is no better way to embellish your designs than to use beads. The sheer variety of shapes and sizes, colours and finishes are a constant source of delight. If you are a beader or just love crafting,

you are sure to enjoy creating any of these stunning designs. The book is divided into two chapters: Decorating for Christmas – full of unique ideas for making your home look extra special, and Giving at Christmas – filled with stunning gifts, wrapping ideas and cards for you to send.

Many of the projects have variations: Fast 'n' Festive are simpler versions of the main project that use quicker methods or simpler materials so they can be completed in much less time, while features called Ring the Changes show an alternative design. Each project has a concise list of what you will need and clear step-by-step instructions to guide you through. Details of the exact beads used in the projects can be found on pages 108–109. At the back of the book there is a section on the materials and equipment you may need, followed by an in-depth techniques section, which gives extra information for those new to beading, so that everyone can join in the fun.

Beads

THE BEAUTY OF BEADS AS A CRAFT MATERIAL IS THEIR DIVERSITY: THERE ARE COLOURS, TEXTURES, SHAPES AND SIZES TO SUIT EVERY PURPOSE AND MUCH OF THE ENJOYMENT COMES FROM SORTING THROUGH THIS WONDERFUL MAZE TO FIND THE EXACT BEADS THAT YOU NEED!

As well as looking for a particular colour or colourway, beads for Christmas decorations or gifts need to have that little bit of sparkle or shine to give the project a festive feel. Glass beads or crystals with facets to catch the light, beads with a silver-lining, metal beads or metallic finishes are all certain to make your beading simply sparkling.

Beads are easier to buy than ever before as there are plenty of craft shops selling beads, lots of suppliers on the Internet or you can source second-hand beads in bric-a-brac shops. look out in the sales for pieces of costume jewellery or beaded items to recycle.

BEAD SIZES

When you hand pick beads it isn't essential to know the exact size, as you can mix and match on the spot, but if you are buying on-line or from a catalogue the beads may not be shown actual size and so it is useful to know how different beads are measured.

Most beads are measured in millimetres. The length and width of long or drop shapes are usually given or for round beads the measurement is across the diameter. Seed beads have their own measurement system that should relate to the number of beads per 2.5cm (1in). The seed beads aren't measured on a string but are laid side by side with the holes facing up. It is not very accurate but does give an indication of the size. The smallest are called petite beads and the most common size range is 9–11, which are 2–2.5mm in diameter. Bugle beads are measured by length.

BEAD HOLES

All beads, apart from accent beads, have holes. Do check before buying that the hole is where you want it – if it is a drop bead the hole may go right through the centre from top to bottom – ideal for a headpin, or there may be a hole near the top. Some beads have holes that are off centre and others, such as flower beads, have a hole going through the back rather like a button with a shank.

Seed beads

Seed beads or rocailles are the group names given to small glass beads, which come in a wide range of sizes, types and quality. Most of the highest quality beads are made in Japan and the Czech Republic and these are the most regular in size and shape. Delicas or antiques are very uniform cylinder-shaped seed beads that are ideal for bead weaving or bead stitches. Rather than the doughnut shape of normal seed beads, cylinder beads have a flat end so that they sit uniformly side by side. Finishes such as frosted and metallic are particularly festive as are silver-lined seed beads, which add extra sparkle to the pompom light garland on page 48.

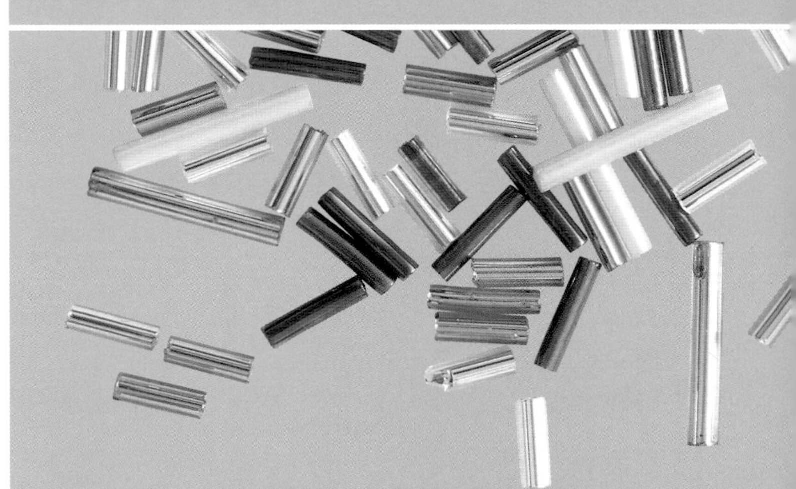

Bugles

Bugles are long cylinder-shaped beads made from rods of glass. They are available straight or twisted in lengths from a few millimetres, known as bugle beads, to over 2.5cm (1in) and come in the same range of colours and finishes as seed beads. The Christmas roses on page 24 use bugles for the flower centres and to add an interesting texture on the fringing.

Crystals

Christmas wouldn't be the same without crystals as they sparkle so seductively, especially in candlelight. Use the finest quality Swarovski crystals for the cracker decorations on page 86 because these gorgeous bead motifs are designed to be kept and used as a piece of jewellery. On the other hand, inexpensive facetted glass beads are ideal to make the beautiful beaded stocking border on page 54 when quantity rather than quality ups the shine factor. Look out for wonderful crystal shapes such as flowers, drops, hearts and cubes, all available in a wide range of colours and sizes.

Pressed glass

Large glass beads are usually pressed in moulds to create lots of different shapes, from leaves and flowers to discs, cylinders and drops. Choose transparent, brightly coloured glass beads that will let the light through to keep your festive projects looking fresh and contemporary, or try opaque, darker shades for a more traditional look. A frosted finish on glass beads, like those used for the pompom lights on page 48, catches the light even more.

Metallic-lined beads

The holes in transparent beads can be lined with gold, silver or another metallic colour to create a beautiful sparkly effect that shines through the glass surround. The metallic lining looks a little like leaf metal and can be flecked or plain. Silver-lined seed beads and bugles are ideal for Christmas projects or use large beads like those used for the wrapping embellishment on page 82.

Pearls

The lustre on pearls takes them into the luxury look even if the beads themselves can be inexpensive. Like every other type of bead the price varies with the quality and so you can make fun decorations, such as the snowflakes on page 14 or the pearl twists on page 44, with plastic beads, or look for quality pearls for a piece of jewellery or special gift.

Lampwork and other decorative beads

All the beads in this group have a metallic lustre on the outside or specks of gold or silver inside the glass, which makes them ideal for the festive season. They include handmade lampwork beads with their distinctive lines of glass wound around the outside. These eye-catching beads are ideal to create a focal point for Christmas jewellery or to make interesting decorations.

Metal beads

Mix gold or silver beads with any colour and you have an instant festive look. Some 'metal' beads are actually painted plastic but look authentic – they even have the advantage of a lighter weight. Look for Christmas shapes like snowflakes, fairies or even little parcels to add a fun touch, or use simpler metal shapes such as rings and washers as spacers to co-ordinate with a mix of different beads, like the subtle gold beads used in the jewellery set on page 72.

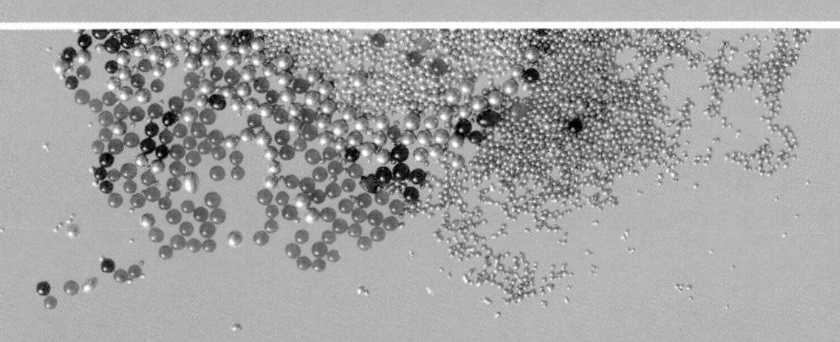

Accent beads

Accent beads are tiny no-hole beads that are stuck on to the background rather than attached with thread. The beads are available in a wide range of colours and are often used in conjunction with seed and bugle beads. The cards on page 78 give you some idea of how great they can look. Double-sided adhesive tape in sheet form can be cut into lots of different shapes and is the cleanest and neatest way to stick the beads. Always begin with the larger beads first and work down to the medium and then fine accent beads.

Colours for Christmas

Making gifts or decorating for Christmas is all about creating a festive look and it is essential to choose particular colours or styles of beads otherwise your efforts could be suitable for any occasion at any time of the year. It is possible to add gold or silver to almost any colour to achieve a festive look but most of the colours associated with Christmas have been chosen for symbolic reasons or to co-ordinate with the seasons. Red and green, from the evergreen leaves and bright red berries of the holly bush, are the most traditional, while blue, white and silver associated with wintry icicles, snowflakes and snow, have a more contemporary feel.

CHOOSING COLOURS

The Christmas look comes from choosing particular colours to create the desired atmosphere. It isn't just about using red and green beads or blue and white – you need to think about the shade of beads that you choose. Colours with an equal depth will harmonize together, such as bright red and bright green for a traditional look, and pink and mint or raspberry and lime for a younger, modern appearance. When decorating for Christmas don't mix the different colourways or the effect will just become muddy, like mixing lots of paints together in a tray – you always end up with brown!

CREATING AN IMPACT

Colours that work well together create more impact and sometimes the simpler colour schemes are the most effective. Red and white has a clean, crisp look, combining the warmth of the reds with wintry white to create a Scandinavian style – used to great effect for the advent calendar on page 30. White with silver and crystal is a really elegant colour scheme that works wonderfully for projects like the Christmas stocking on page 54 and the candle embellishments on page 36.

Multicolour schemes can be really stunning, though their success depends on getting exactly the right shades in each colour. The Oriental look is very rich and warm, using bright blue, fuchsia, orange and lime to contrast with a deep purple. These colours work equally well with either gold or silver and look stunning made into a Christmas stocking for the children (page 59) or for a set of night light holders (page 18).

Whatever colour you choose remember that unless it is a gift, the colours have to work with the décor in your home. If you think of a colour wheel, the colours that harmonize are next to each other, and the colours that contrast are on opposite sides of the wheel. In fact the rules for decorating at Christmas are just the same as you would apply for buying soft furnishings. Generally, you want things to match or tone but sometimes a few well-placed items in a strong contrast colour make the biggest impact.

Ice Blue
'Cold as ice' and 'blue with the cold' are just two expressions that epitomize this particular colour scheme. But blue and white beads could quite easily be ideal for summer (think beach-hut style), so to make it really wintry choose transparent pale blues and bright whites to keep everything looking distinctly chilly – a few silver beads add a little depth.

Raspberry Ripple

Choose transparent or frosted beads with pretty, shapes in raspberry and lime to create a fresh and clean look that is really contemporary. These two colours really exude luxury and will certainly brighten up the festivities. For an alternative modern look, try pale pink and mint, which also looks wonderful mixed with a few silver beads.

White Christmas

All white can be simply stunning at Christmas time. White beads are highly reflective and so an all-white scheme can look too uniform. To break the monotony use an assortment of white beads with different finishes, such as frosted, transparent and ceylon, or add a little warmth with champagne-coloured beads while still maintaining the cool effect.

Sparkling Splendour

Deep purple works wonderfully with gold. Look out for purple beads that have been speckled with gold or luxurious lampwork beads to create a really opulent effect and to pull the whole design together. Burgundy and gold also work well but burgundy can be a little dark and gloomy so add a few pink or raspberry beads to lift the design.

Berries and Leaves

Red and green are the traditional Christmas colours, reflecting the evergreen leaves and bright red berries that are so abundant at this time of year. Choose the brightest red and freshest green beads for a really luscious look. Metallics always add to the festive spirit, so try a splash of gold with either red or green for a really stunning effect.

23
7
8

DECORATING FOR CHRISTMAS

Let it snow

PEOPLE SAY THAT NO TWO SNOWFLAKES ARE ALIKE, BUT HOW DO THEY KNOW? APART FROM A CHANGE OF COLOURWAY THESE DELICIOUSLY DELICATE SNOWFLAKE DECORATIONS ARE ALL THE SAME, BUT YOU COULD MAKE EACH ONE SLIGHTLY DIFFERENT SO THAT CHILDREN OR GUESTS CAN HAVE FUN SPOTTING THE DIFFERENCE! TRY CHANGING THE ORDER OF THE BEADS ON THE PRE-FORMED WIRE SHAPE OR EXPERIMENTING WITH THE SEED BEAD DETAIL, MAKING SUBTLE CHANGES TO THE STEMS AND BRANCHES SO THAT EACH DECORATION IS UNIQUE.

CHOOSE CRYSTALS AND METAL BEADS to catch the light as the snowflakes dangle from the Christmas tree and create a gorgeous antique feel by fitting silver-plated filigree caps at both ends of the pearls.

SEED BEAD BRANCHES are made individually using fine silver-plated wire and attached to the main snowflake decoration, with a medium crystal added in the centre to finish. For a simpler look, you can leave the snowflakes plain without a central seed bead motif.

SIMPLE ICICLE DROPLETS can be made in next to no time – the ideal project if you are short of time or simply want to vary the shape and style of the decorations. See page 17 for making up instructions.

Beaded snowflakes

YOU WILL NEED (for one decoration)

• Snowflake wire 15cm (6in) • Round pearls: twelve 6mm, six 8mm and six 10mm, all pale blue • Round crystals: seven 6mm, six 8mm and six 10mm, all aquamarine • Round grooved metal beads: six 8mm and six 10mm • Seed beads size 9 (2.5mm), 15g colour-lined or silver-lined • Filigree caps, twelve 7mm • Filigree caps, twelve 10mm • Bead glue • Silver-plated wire 0.315mm (30swg)

1 On one stem of the snowflake wire pick up a 6mm crystal, 6mm pearl, 8mm grooved bead, 7mm filigree cap, 8mm pearl, 7mm filigree cap, 10mm pearl, 10mm grooved bead, 10mm filigree cap, 10mm pearl, 10mm filigree cap and an 8mm crystal. Apply a little glue to the end of the wire stem and then push on the final 6mm pearl.

2 Miss a stem then repeat the sequence on the next stem. Fill a third stem in the same way. To fill two other stems pick up a 6mm pearl, 8mm crystal, 10mm grooved bead, 10mm filigree cap, 10mm pearl, 10mm filigree cap, 10mm crystal, 8mm grooved bead, 7mm filigree cap, 8mm pearl, 7mm filigree cap, 6mm pearl and then stick a 6mm pearl at the end.

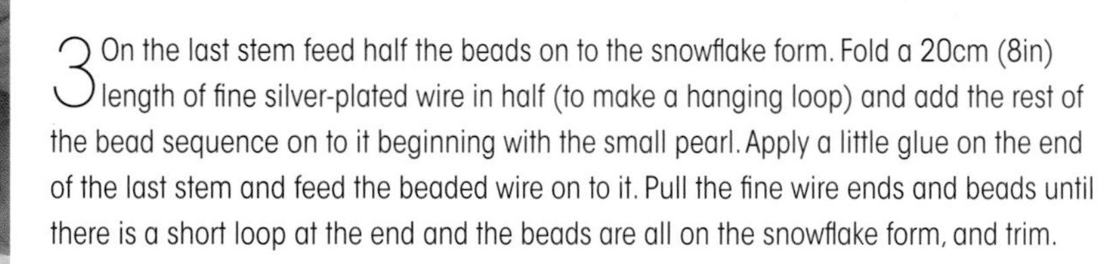

3 On the last stem feed half the beads on to the snowflake form. Fold a 20cm (8in) length of fine silver-plated wire in half (to make a hanging loop) and add the rest of the bead sequence on to it beginning with the small pearl. Apply a little glue on the end of the last stem and feed the beaded wire on to it. Pull the fine wire ends and beads until there is a short loop at the end and the beads are all on the snowflake form, and trim.

4 To make the seed bead embellishment in the centre of the snowflake, cut a 36cm (14in) length of wire and twist a small loop on one end. Pick up 25 seed beads and drop them down until they are about 5cm (2in) from the loop. Holding the long tail of the wire, miss the end bead and feed the wire through the next 3 beads. Pick up 4 beads and let them drop down to the stem. Miss the end bead and feed the wire through the next 3 beads – this makes the first branch.

5 Feed the wire down through the next 4 beads on the stem and make two six-bead branches. Feed the wire down through the next 6 beads on the stem and make two eight-bead branches. Feed the wire down through the last beads on the stem. Make six long snowflake stems in total.

Check that the beads you are using have a large enough hole to feed through a double length of 0.315mm (30swg) wire fairly easily.

6 Wrap the wire ends around each stem near the centre of the snowflake. Make six shorter snowflake stems for the centre by picking up 14 seed beads to begin and then repeating the first part of the larger snowflake stem until there are two six-bead branches. Take the tail wire through the remaining beads on the stem to complete. Feed the wires of these snowflake stems into the centre of the snowflake decoration and twist all the wires together on the reverse side to secure.

7 Trim the wires neatly and push the end flat against the decoration. Finally, feed a 6mm crystal on to a length of fine wire. Tie it across the centre of the snowflake decoration, twist the wires together at the back and trim neatly.

Pre-formed snowflake wires are available in a range of sizes so you can choose the size to suit your Christmas tree, perhaps making a large snowflake for the top of the tree and smaller decorations for hanging.

Fast 'n' festive

ICICLE DROPLETS

To make these stylish icicle droplets you will need: 0.8mm (21swg) silver-plated wire; round-nosed pliers; a few pearls, crystals and metallic beads in graduated sizes; filigree caps; bead glue.

Cut 15cm (6in) of the wire and make a loop at one end with the pliers. Coil the end round by hand to make a 1.5cm (⅝in) circle. Bend the tail of the wire at a right angle next to the coil. Add the beads, beginning with the largest pearl and filigree caps and finishing with the smallest crystal. Trim the end of the wire flush with the crystal and then remove it temporarily to apply a little beading glue. Leave to dry and then hang the loop over a branch of the Christmas tree.

We three kings

TALL CANDLES CAN SOMETIMES GET IN THE WAY AT CHRISTMAS, ESPECIALLY IF THERE ARE LOTS OF GUESTS AROUND THE TABLE AND SERVING DISHES TO BE PASSED AROUND, AND THAT IS WHERE THESE EXQUISITE LITTLE TEALIGHT HOLDERS COME INTO THEIR OWN. THEY CAN OF COURSE BE USED OVER AND OVER AGAIN AND AS EACH ONE LOOKS LIKE A LITTLE CROWN FIT FOR A KING, THEY'LL DEFINITELY CREATE THE RIGHT ATMOSPHERE. THE DELIGHTFUL ZIGZAG TEXTURE IS CREATED BY HERRINGBONE STITCH, WHICH IS QUICK TO WORK AS YOU ADD TWO BEADS AT A TIME AND THE CIRCULAR DESIGN IS EVEN EASIER TO WORK THAN FLAT BEADED FABRIC!

TWO TONES OF BEADS add a vibrant edging to the crown shape. Use pretty little star beads for a fun design or use Swarovski crystals that will really sparkle.

ADD A PRETTY FRILLED EDGE around the top of the holder to make a simple but effective edging to the basic design. Use silver-lined beads that will sparkle in the candlelight.

HEX AND SILVER-LINED BEADS have contrasting textures that really work together on these little tealight holders. Choose beads in the same size so you can change from one to the other easily.

Hex tealight

YOU WILL NEED (for one tealight)

- Silver-lined (s-l) seed beads, size 9 (2.5mm), 10g lilac • Hex beads, size 9 (2.5mm), 10g lilac
- Bicone crystals 6mm, twelve each in lilac and fuchsia • Nymo thread • Beading needle size 10

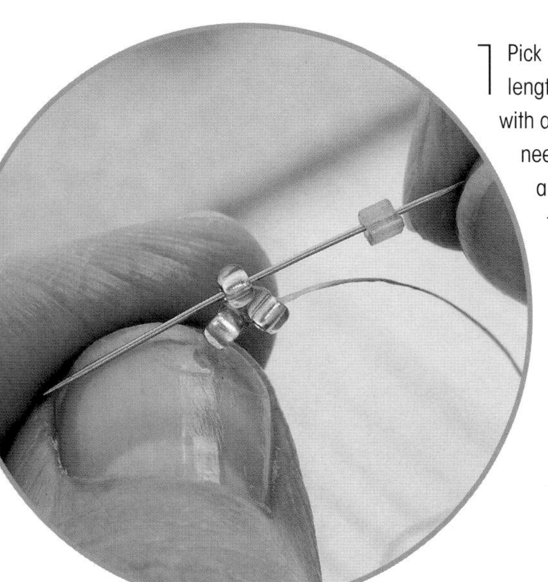

1 Pick up 3 silver-lined beads on a 1m (1yd) length of Nymo thread, tie together in a circle with a reef knot (see page 100) and pass the needle back through the first bead. * Pick up a hex bead and pass the needle through the next silver-lined (s-l) bead. Repeat from * to add 2 more hex beads.

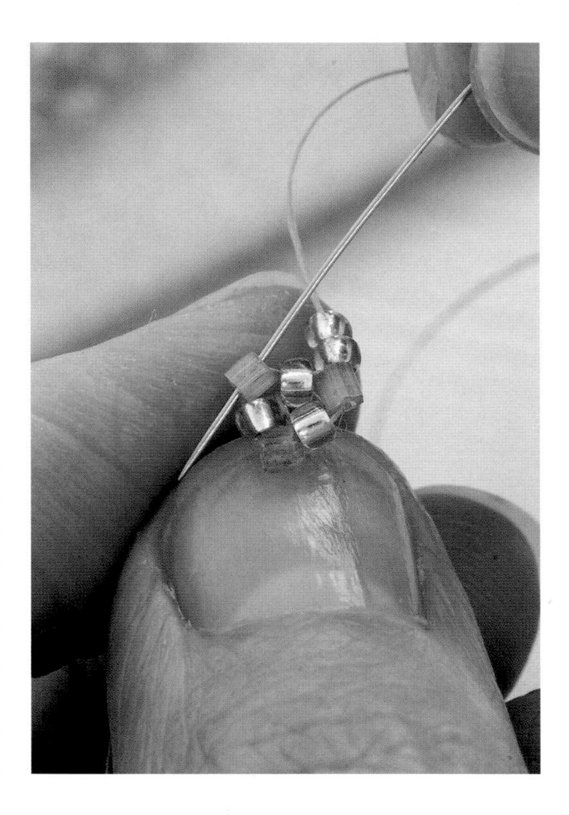

2 * Pass the needle through the next hex bead and pick up 2 s-l beads. Repeat from * twice more. This forms the foundation of the tealight before you begin herringbone stitch and is shown on the beading diagram below by the inner black ring.

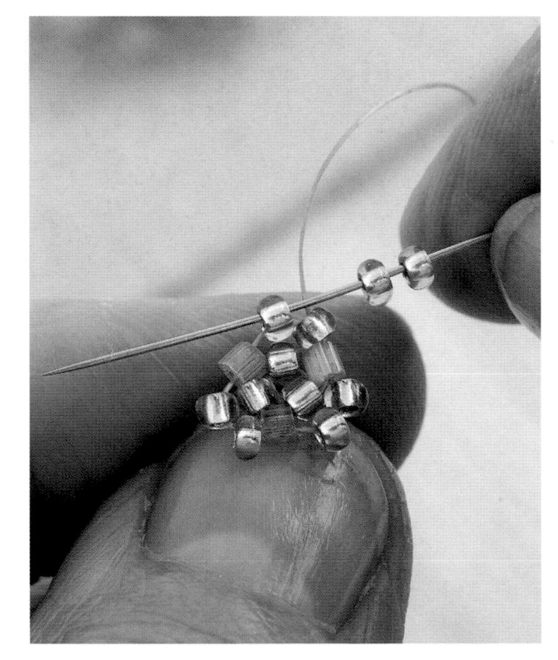

3 * Pass the needle through the next s-l bead. Referring to the beading diagram, begin to work the herringbone stitch (see opposite), picking up 2 s-l beads and taking the needle back through the next s-l bead. Pick up 2 hex beads. Repeat from * twice to complete the round.

Hex tealight beading diagram – base only
Inner black ring = beading done by end of step 2
Middle black ring = beading done by end of step 4
Outer black ring = beading done by end of step 6

4 In order to make the flat circular base of the tealight holder you need to keep increasing and 'picking up' beads between herringbone stitches achieves this. Add 1 bead in the first round and 2 in the second round and then you can work a herringbone stitch into these two beads in the third round, as follows: * work 1 s-l herringbone stitch, pick up 1 s-l bead, work 1 hex herringbone stitch, pick up 1 s-l bead. Repeat from * twice. You should now be at the middle black circle on the diagram, with 24 beads on the outer row.

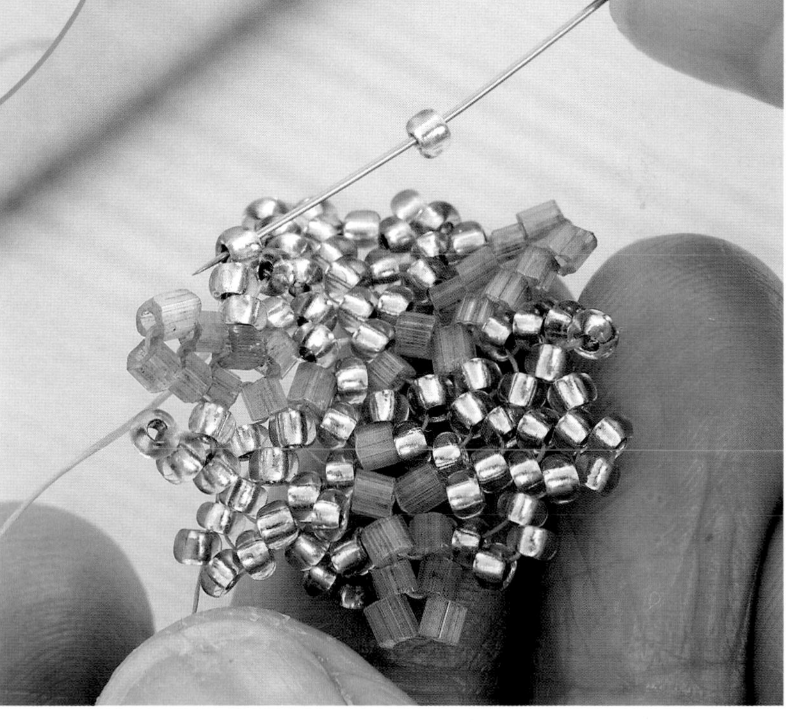

5 * Work 1 s-l herringbone stitch, pick up 2 s-l beads, work 1 hex herringbone stitch, pick up 2 s-l beads. Repeat from * twice. Next round work herringbone stitch all round keeping the contrast pattern going.

Herringbone stitch
The diagram illustrates the path of the thread through the previous row of beads

The tension and firmness of the bead fabric depends on how tightly you work the stitches. If the thread is too loose the sides of the containers will not support the decorative edge.

6 Next round, work 1 herringbone stitch and add 1 s-l bead. Repeat all round keeping the contrast pattern going. Next round work 1 herringbone stitch and add 2 s-l beads. Repeat all round keeping the contrast pattern going. Next round work herringbone stitch all round keeping the contrast pattern going. You should have 48 beads on the outer row and be at the outer ring on the diagram – this completes the base of the tealight.

Remember that candles should never be left unattended when lit.

7 For the next eight rounds work herringbone stitch using silver-lined beads only. Keep the stitches tight and after a couple of rounds the sides of the tea light holder will begin to stand straight. For the next three rounds work herringbone stitch using hex beads only. If you want to make a taller tealight holder add extra rounds at this stage.

8 To make the shaped edge at the top of the tealight holder begin to increase the beads as follows: next round continue working the herringbone stitch with hex beads and add 1 silver-lined bead between each stitch. Next round add 2 s-l beads between each stitch.

9 Next round * take the needle through the next 2 hex beads ready to work herringbone stitch. Pick up a hex bead, a bicone crystal and s-l seed bead. Take the needle back through the bicone crystal and the hex bead. Feed the needle down the next 2 hex beads and up between the next 2 silver-lined beads. Add a bicone crystal and s-l seed bead. Take the needle through the crystal and the next s-l seed bead. Repeat from * all the way round.

10 Make two more tealight holders by following steps 1–8 and using different coloured beads. Work alternative edgings as described in the Ring the Changes panel, below.

Ring the changes

STARRY NIGHT

For this pretty amber version of the tealight holder, change the lilac hex beads to orange and work as in steps 1–8 on pages 20–22. Now continue to work the fringe as follows.

Next round * take the needle through the next 2 hex beads ready to work herringbone stitch. Pick up a dark orange star bead and a silver-lined seed bead. Take the needle back through the dark orange star and the next hex bead. Feed the needle down the hex beads and through the next 2 silver-lined beads. On the next 2 hex beads pick up a hex bead before you add a pale orange star bead and then add another hex bead after you pass the needle back through the star again. Alternating the two star colours, repeat from * all the way round to finish.

FRILLY DELIGHT

To create this delicate green version of the tealight holder, change the lilac hex beads to mint and work as in steps 1–8 on pages 20–22. Now continue to work the frilled edge as follows.

Next round, work herringbone stitch all round using only silver-lined beads. Next round, work herringbone stitch adding 1 s-l bead between each stitch.

Fleurs de noel

USUALLY THERE IS NOTHING TO BEAT THE REAL THING BUT THESE EXQUISITE BEADED FLOWERS ARE SIMPLY STUNNING AND LOOK ABSOLUTELY FANTASTIC BALANCED SO DELIGHTFULLY ON A BEAUTIFUL CHRISTMAS BAUBLE. THE TECHNIQUE KNOWN AS FRENCH BEADING, WHERE SHAPES ARE CREATED USING BEADED WIRE BENT AROUND A CENTRE ROW OF BEADS FLOWERS, WAS POPULAR IN VICTORIAN TIMES AND IS SURPRISINGLY QUICK AND EASY. MAKE THESE ELEGANT CHRISTMAS ROSES OR, IF TIME IS OF THE ESSENCE, TRY THE MISTLETOE ON PAGE 29.

RIBBONS AND PRETTY CORDS add a softness and delicacy to the beaded decoration. Tie the ribbons around the decoration or tie the ribbon in bows and attach around the flowers with a low-melt glue gun.

INTRICATE DETAILS like the pretty coloured centres in the Christmas roses make the flowers look more realistic. Use coloured enamelled wire for an authentic look and a variety of beads to create interesting textures.

SILVER-LINED BUGLES add a touch of sparkle in the dangling bead fringe. Mix bugles and seed beads to add interest and alter the lengths of each strand for a more natural look.

Beaded blossoms

YOU WILL NEED

• Short bugles 15g white • Bugles 7mm 15g green • Seed beads size 11 (2mm) 5g yellow and 5g green
• White wire, 5m (5yd) of 0.4mm (27swg) • Green wire, 2m (2yd) of 0.4mm (27swg) • Green florist's tape
• Green quilting thread • Christmas bauble • Gauze ribbon and decorative cord 1m (1yd) of each
• Low-melt glue gun

1 To make a petal, work directly off the reel of white wire, picking up 36cm (14in) of short bugles. Make a small loop on the end of the wire to prevent the beads falling off. Drop 8 short bugles down to the loop. Leave a tail of 8cm (3in) and then wrap the wire around four fingers and twist about five or six times to make a large loop. These short bugles will form the centre row of the petal.

2 Bring the long string of beads up beside the centre row. Drop 8 short bugles down the large loop and move the rest of the beads to the end of the wire tail. Hold the working wire at 90° and wind it around the centre wire once. Bring another 8 or 9 beads down the working wire and repeat the winding sequence at the bottom of the petal.

3 Keep working from top to bottom adding 1–2 beads each time until you begin to create the petal shape. After nine rows of beads are added, change the angle of the wire at the top of the petal slightly to 45° to make a slightly pointed end.

4 Wrap the wire tightly around the stem after the 11th row and trim. Trim the centre wire to 6mm (¼in) and bend it over to the reverse side. Make five petals in total and put aside.

Make a loop at the end of the wire to stop the beads falling off and to prevent it poking your eye.

5 To make the stamens, pick up 18 yellow seed beads on white wire straight off the reel. Bend the wire about 3cm (1¼in) from the end so that one bead is where the wire bends. Hold the bead and twist the wire for about 1cm (½in). Tighten the twist by holding the bead in flat-nosed pliers and turning a few times. Keep making stamens until all the beads are used.

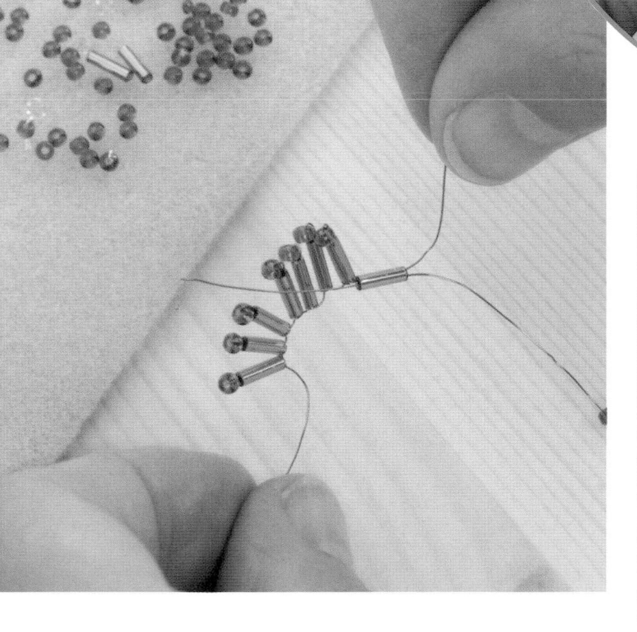

6 To make the green centre, pick up a green bugle and a seed bead on green wire. Feed the wire back down through the bugle and pull tight so that the seed bead ends up on the end. Repeat thirteen times.

7 Assemble the flower by wrapping the green bugles around the yellow stamens and arrange attractively. Position the flower petals around the flower centre and twist all the wires together to make the stem. Make a second flower in the same way for each decoration.

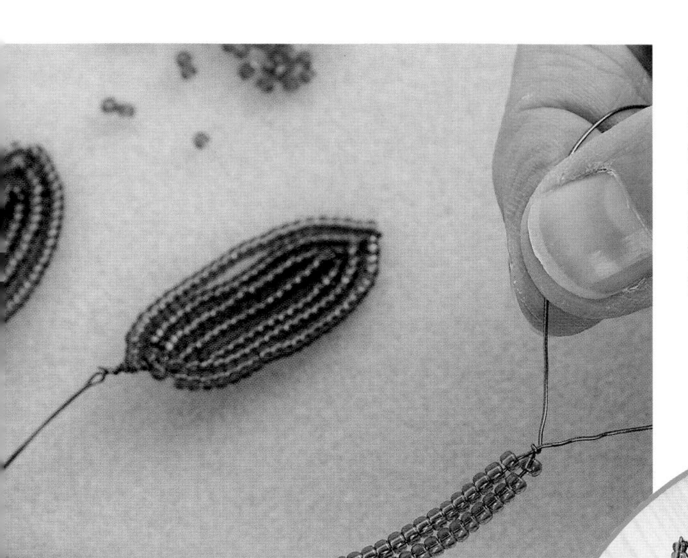

8 To make the leaves, pick up 25cm (10in) of green seed beads on to the green wire straight off the reel. Make a small loop on the end and drop 16 beads down to the loop. Make a loop around four fingers as before and twist. Make the leaves in the same way as the petals although with only seven bead rows so that they are a longer, narrow shape. Make three leaves for each decoration.

9 Hold two leaves behind one of the beaded flowers and wrap florist's tape around the wires to make a stem. Begin just beneath the petals and fold the ends of the wire over to make a short stem. Wrap the remaining leaf behind the second flower. Hold both flowers together and wrap the stems together to make a small spray. Depending on the shape of the bauble, you may need a third flower and more leaves to balance the decoration.

If you don't have a strong thread like quilting thread, use two strands of sewing thread in the needle to make the bead fringing.

10 Make some fringe strands to hang down below the flowers on the decoration. Pick up alternate seed beads and bugles on a long length of quilting thread until there are about 15 bugles. Leave the last seed bead and take the needle back up the bead strand. Make about six bugle strands and another five or six seed bead strands, all slightly different lengths.

11 Make a loop of wire to fit over the top of the decoration. Tie the beaded strands to the loop and trim the excess thread. Loop the wire over the bauble and secure with a few dots of glue from a low-melt glue gun.

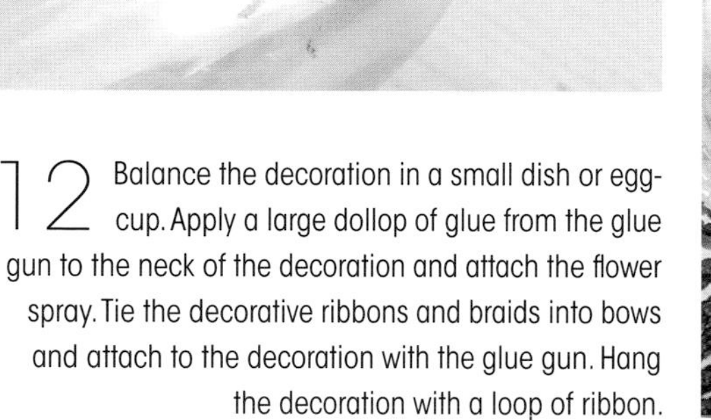

12 Balance the decoration in a small dish or egg-cup. Apply a large dollop of glue from the glue gun to the neck of the decoration and attach the flower spray. Tie the decorative ribbons and braids into bows and attach to the decoration with the glue gun. Hang the decoration with a loop of ribbon.

Fast 'n' festive

CHRISTMAS KISSES

Hang a few of these beaded decorations above a doorway to create some Christmas fun. To make the mistletoe you will need: silver-lined green seed beads size 9 (2.5mm); 6mm and 8mm white pearls; dark green wire 0.45mm (26swg); a glass bauble; decorative ribbon.

Begin in the same way as for the Christmas rose leaves (step 8) but with 15 seed beads on the centre row. Add about 18 seed beads on the next two rows to make the leaf. For each spray of mistletoe make six leaves. Twist three pairs together leaving 1cm (½in) stems and then twist two branches together for 1cm (½in). Leave one long wire at the join and twist the rest of the wires tightly. Make the mistletoe berries by feeding the wire through a pearl, picking up a seed bead and going back through the pearl. Add 3 small and 1 large pearl. Add the third pair of leaves part-way down the main spray stem and attach berries as before. Make two mistletoe sprays for each bauble, attach with a glue gun and decorate with ribbons to finish.

Countdown to Christmas

HATS, MITTENS AND STOCKINGS ARE JUST WHAT YOU NEED TO KEEP WARM IN THE WINTER AND THESE COSY LITTLE ITEMS WILL HELP MAKE YOUR HOME WARM AND INVITING TOO. STRUNG UP ON A CORD ACROSS THE MANTELPIECE OR USED TO DECORATE THE TREE, THESE PARTICULAR CHRISTMAS SHAPES HAVE BEEN CHOSEN BECAUSE THEY CAN BE MADE WITH AN OPENING AT THE TOP FOR LITTLE GIFTS OR MESSAGES. IF TRADITIONAL IS NOT YOUR STYLE, CHECK OUT THE SWEET TREATS ON PAGE 35 FOR A FUN CONTEMPORARY LOOK INSTEAD.

TINY GOLDEN BELLS add a little Christmas cheer to these delightful felt shapes. Children will love shaking the cord to jingle the bells. Tie bells along the hanging cord too for even more impact.

WHITE EMBROIDERY ON RED FELT is traditional in Scandinavian countries at Christmas time. Add texture with tiny, opaque white seed beads incorporated into the embroidery stitches. Use your imagination to make each stocking, mitten and hat slightly different.

BEADED NUMBERS stitched on the cuff of each shape turn simple decorations into an unusual Advent calendar – each shape has an opening at the top for a tiny gift, message or candy cane to keep everyone amused right up to the big day.

23
7
3
18
6
4
8
15
1

Advent garland

YOU WILL NEED (for the whole garland of twenty-four)

- Red felt, 1.25m ($1\frac{1}{3}$yd) x 91cm (36in) wide • White and red stranded cotton (floss)
- Seed beads, size 11 (2mm) 15g white opaque • Ball beads, 7mm ($\frac{3}{8}$in), forty-eight white
- Narrow white satin ribbon 1m (1yd) • Small gold bells, twenty-four

1 Trace the mitten, hat and stocking shapes on page 105 on to white paper and cut out. Trace and cut out the cuff shapes on separate pieces of paper. Pin the stocking shape on to a double layer of red felt and cut out. Cut one cuff shape. To make an advent garland you will need twenty-four finished items, so cut out eight sets of each shape.

Use felt scraps and leftover beads to make individual decorations for the Christmas tree. To make a set of three you would need a piece of felt 30 x 45cm (12 x 18in).

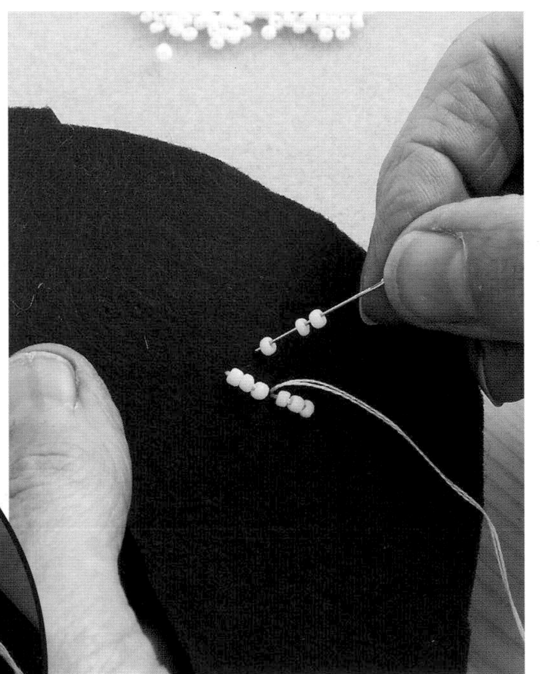

2 Using two strands of white embroidery thread, secure the thread on the reverse side and bring it out in the middle of one of the stocking shapes (see Techniques page 98). Pick up 3 white seed beads and take the needle back through about 7mm ($\frac{3}{8}$in) further up. Make four more beaded straight stitches to make a simple star.

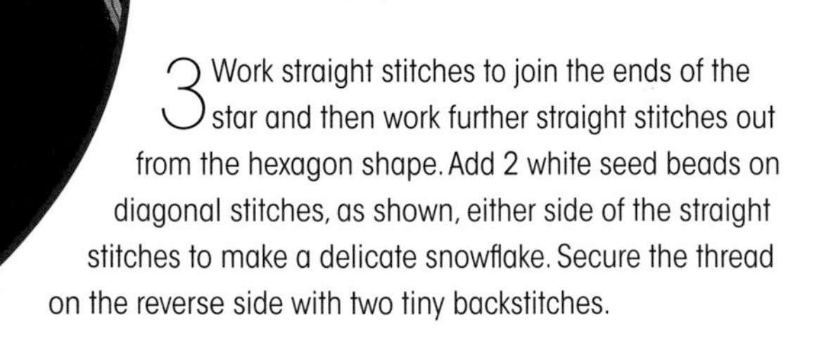

3 Work straight stitches to join the ends of the star and then work further straight stitches out from the hexagon shape. Add 2 white seed beads on diagonal stitches, as shown, either side of the straight stitches to make a delicate snowflake. Secure the thread on the reverse side with two tiny backstitches.

If you want to use the felt shapes purely as a garland, omit the numbers and add extra beaded embroidery motifs on the cuff.

4 Draw a number on the cuff section of the stocking with a pencil (see page 105 for numbers to trace). Couch white seed beads along the line (see page 99). Work two small snowflake shapes on either side of the number, adding beads as shown. When the number is a double digit you can stitch smaller designs on either side.

5 Pin the cuff on to the embroidered stocking shape. Bring a single strand of red embroidery thread out at the bottom edge of the cuff. Pick up 3 white seed beads, work a buttonhole stitch and pull the stitch taut, so that the beads are along the edge of the cuff (see page 100). Continue along the edge with beaded buttonhole stitch.

Strengthen the opening of the stocking by oversewing the ends of the threads at the top of the cuff on each side.

6 Turn the embroidered stocking over and cut off the excess felt from the top edge of the stocking shape under the cuff. Pin the remaining stocking section on the back and then, with a single strand of red embroidery thread, work buttonhole stitch around the edge.

7 Thread 2 white ball beads on to narrow satin ribbon. Tie a simple overhand knot (see page 100) at one end and then leave a gap of 2.5–3cm (1–1¼in) between the beads and tie another knot. Manoeuvre the knot to the right place using the blunt end of a needle. Trim the ends of the ribbon and then fold in half and sew invisibly under the cuff.

8 The other shapes are made up in the same way by cutting two main shapes and one cuff shape. An alternative decoration for the hat is to make a pretty line design. Mark the felt with guidelines using a large needle and work rows of backstitch across the felt shape. Embroider diagonal lines of 3 seed beads at each stitch end. Once the hat is made up, sew a bell on the pointed end.

9 Small snowflakes make an attractive all-over design for any of the shapes. Make the required number of felt shapes, making sure that you put a different number on each one if it is for an advent calendar. Vary the designs of the snowflakes and other motifs, perhaps making toe and heel shapes for a variation and also putting the number on the main part of the felt shape for a change. Pin the shapes on to a cord to display as a garland.

Ring the changes

SWEET TREAT GARLAND

One of the wonderful things about Christmas is the abundance of good food and lovely treats but if you don't want to buy too many goodies try stitching a few instead! You will need: scraps of pink, blue, yellow and brown felt; bugle beads and sequins in assorted colours; matching sewing threads, ribbon and miniature metallic pegs to hang.

Use the templates on page 104 to cut two of each shape from felt and then add beads, sequins and embroidery to one of each shape as shown in the photo opposite. Sew a plain felt shape to each embroidered motif using buttonhole stitch around the edge. If you want to make your gingerbread men, cupcakes and candy canes a little plumper, fill with polyester stuffing or cut a smaller felt shape to fit inside before stitching all the way around the edge.

Enchanting candlelight

NO TABLE AT CHRISTMAS WOULD BE COMPLETE WITHOUT CANDLES. THEY CREATE A WONDERFULLY COSY ATMOSPHERE AND IF YOU LIVE IN CHILLIER CLIMES, LET YOU FORGET THE COLD WEATHER OUTSIDE. ONCE THEY HAVE BEEN USED, HOWEVER, CANDLES DON'T LOOK AS ATTRACTIVE BUT THESE PRETTY BEAD DROPLETS CAN BE RECYCLED – THEY ARE PINNED INTO THE CANDLE AND CAN BE REMOVED AND STORED AWAY UNTIL THE NEXT SPECIAL EVENT, CHANGING THE CANDLE COLOUR TO SUIT THE OCCASION.

LARGE DROP BEADS add weight to the bottom of the bead embellishment. Work up the charm using slightly smaller beads or fewer beads in each charm to create a balanced look.

SEQUINS AND METAL BEADS make a simpler variation. Use brightly coloured, round sequins for a 60s look (see page 39) or try star-shaped sequins in silver or gold for classic style.

FINE SILVER CHAIN draped elegantly between the bead embellishments links them together and creates a design that can be viewed from any direction. Use shortened headpins to attach the beads and chain and transfer to a new candle when necessary.

Chainlink candle droplets

YOU WILL NEED (for one candle with four droplets)

• Clear crystal or glass drop beads 15–20mm, four • Mixed clear crystal and silver beads 4–12mm, fifty • Metallic silver ring beads 6mm, sixteen • Silver-plated headpins • Silver-plated chain in fine (60cm) and medium weights (20cm) • Silver-plated decorative or triangle bails • Jump rings • Jewellery tools • Tall candle about 7cm (2¾in) in diameter

1 Collect together a selection of crystal, clear glass and silver metallic beads. Choose some beads that have a hole at the top to attach to the bottom of the droplet. Cut a 5cm (2in) length of the medium-weight silver-plated chain by cutting through one of the links with wire cutters.

2 To attach beads with a hole at the top, use a triangle or decorative bail. Open the bail, insert the bead and then squeeze with flat-nosed pliers to secure. Open a jump ring (see Techniques page 102) and attach the bail to the last link. Attach small beads such as tiny teardrops, using a jump ring. Open the ring and feed on the teardrop, and attach to the jump ring above the bail.

If the bead is quite thin, trim a little off the lugs on the bail before fitting, otherwise the end of the bead may break off.

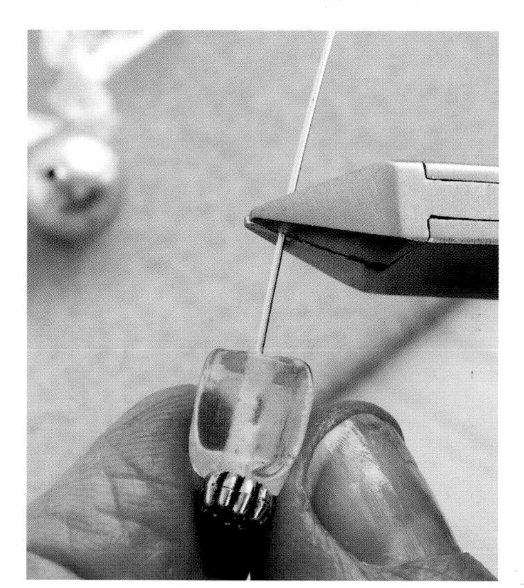

3 Beads with a hole through the middle are attached using a headpin, which is rather like a large dressmaker's pin. Feed the bead on to the headpin and trim the end of the wire to 7–8mm (5/16in). Bend the end into a ring (see Techniques page 102). Open the ring and attach to the next link on the chain.

4 Work up the chain adding beads to each link, alternating the beads from side to side to create a balanced shape. Use larger beads at the bottom of the droplet and make them gradually smaller as you work your way up, adding about 7 large beads and 2 or 3 teardrops. Use two pairs of pliers such as snipe-nosed and round-nosed pliers to open and shut the rings.

5 Attach tiny teardrop beads with a small jump ring. Cut a 6cm (2⅜in) length of silver-plated chain and make a slightly longer droplet. Keep the beads fairly similar, perhaps beginning with a different drop bead at the bottom of the chain. Make two short droplets and two long droplets for each candle.

6 Trim six headpins to 2.5cm (1in). Pick up a metallic ring bead on the first headpin and then one of the longer droplets. Attach two lengths of fine chain and push the headpin into the candle near the top edge.

7 Pick up a metallic ring bead and a shorter droplet on another headpin. Loop one of the fine chains and attach to the headpin, loop the second chain so that it hangs slightly longer and then press the headpin into the candle about 2.5cm (1in) from the top edge. Keep working around the candle until you reach the first droplet again. Pull out the headpin, attach the chain loops and then trim off any excess.

Look out for costume jewellery made from fine and medium-weight silver-plated chain – it's a cheap way to buy chain, especially at sale time.

Fast 'n' festive

SEQUINNED CANDLE

This ball candle is very quick to decorate, with an attractive retro look. To make it you will need: orange, anemone, green, blue and red sequins in 6mm (forty-five), 10mm and 16mm sizes (twenty-five each); large gold seed beads; pincraft pins; 8cm (3in) ball candle.

Pick up a gold bead and a small sequin on a pin through the centre hole and then push the pin through a medium-sized sequin between the hole and the side edge so that the small sequin is off centre. Pick up a large sequin through the centre hole and push the pin into the candle. Continue adding groups of 3 sequins, mixing the colours each time to cover the candle. Add a few single sequins to fill gaps in between.

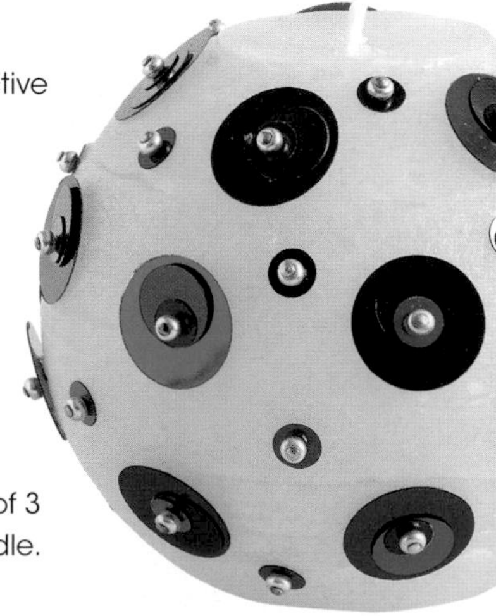

Berry merry Christmas

SOME OF THE BEST IDEAS ARE THE SIMPLEST AND THIS GORGEOUS BEAD GARLAND CERTAINLY FITS THE BILL. IT'S A SIMPLE TECHNIQUE THAT TRANSFORMS INTO SOMETHING QUITE STUNNING WHEN YOU CHOOSE THE RIGHT BEADS IN PRETTY, CO-ORDINATING COLOURS. THE LENGTHS OF BEADED GARLAND CAN BE USED IN DIFFERENT WAYS – WRAP AROUND A NATURAL VINE WREATH, DRAPE ALONG A TABLE OR ARRANGE AROUND A CANDLE IN A TALL CONTAINER AND LET THE ENDS DRAPE DOWN TO CREATE AN EYE-CATCHING CENTREPIECE.

TIE BOWS OF SHEER RIBBON along the twisted wire to soften the effect and add an extra delicacy to the design. Longer ribbons dangling over the edge add a finishing touch.

A BEAD GARLAND makes a stunning napkin ring – perfect if you are short of time or want a co-ordinated Christmas table (see page 43).

PALE PINK AND GREEN PEARLS make a classy and delicate garland for the Christmas table. Adding a few deep pink and dark green pearls amongst the paler pearls really lifts the design.

Garland centrepiece

YOU WILL NEED

- Pale green pearls, fifteen 8mm, fifty 6mm and ninety 4mm • Pink pearls, twenty 8mm and ninety 4mm
- Deep pink pearls twenty 8mm and fifteen 6mm • Dark green pearls twenty 6mm and fifty 4mm
- Translucent leaf-shaped beads 12 x 7mm, 130 • Supa lime wire, 5m (5yd) of 0.5mm (25swg)
- Sheer cream or pink ribbon 1m (1yd) x 7mm (⅜in) wide and 1m (1yd) x 1.5cm (⅝in) wide

1 Cut a 1m (1yd) length of supa lime wire and fold it in half. Pick up a large pale green pearl and drop it down to the centre. Twist the bead until the wire is twisted for about 1cm (½in) to make a stem.

2 Pick up 2 leaf beads on one of the wires and drop down to the centre. Bend the wire around one leaf near the stem and give it one twist to secure. Bend the wire around the other leaf on the other side and twist again to secure. Twist the wire stem for another 1.5cm (⅝in).

3 Pick up a medium deep pink pearl and bend the wire 2cm (¾in) from the stem then twist down to the stem. Continue twisting to make another 1cm (½in) of stem. Pick up 3 small pale pink pearls on one end of the wire. Drop down to 3cm (1¼in) from the stem, cross the wire over to make them into a circle shape and then twist again.

4 Continue down the wires, adding beads and leaves to make a garland with an assortment of different pearl sizes and colours. Add an extra length of wire by starting a new length in the same way as before and then twisting the ends around the new length to join the two pieces together.

Alternate the end of the wire that you add beads on to, so that they both shorten at the same rate.

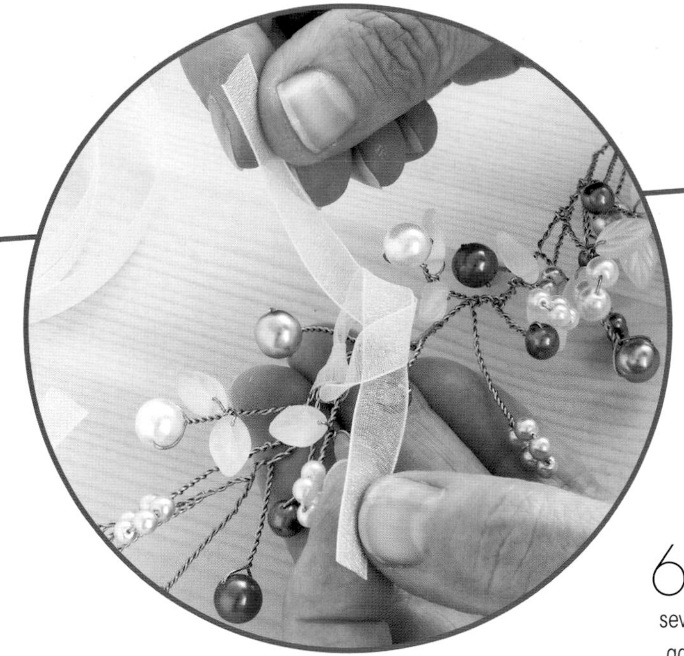

5 Continue making the garland until it is long enough to fit around a large candle. Tie pieces of the narrow sheer ribbon around the garland at intervals and then trim the ends of the ribbons at an angle. Wrap the garland around the candle and secure the ends together so that the join is not obvious.

6 If you have a tall candleholder, make several lengths of bead garland to hang down. Tie lengths of narrow ribbon down each length as before and then attach the individual strands to the wreath by twisting the ends of the wire around securely.

7 To add a little lightness and elegance to the bead garland, tie long lengths of slightly wider sheer ribbon around the wreath and let the ends hang down between the bead strands.

Fast 'n' festive

BEADED NAPKIN RING

Make the Christmas table look extra special by making a set of pretty napkin rings. To make one napkin ring you will need: a selection of pale green, dark green, pink and deep pink pearls in assorted sizes (see page 108 for detailed list); translucent leaf-shaped beads 12 x 7mm; 1m (1yd) of 0.5mm (25swg) supa lime wire; 1m (1yd) x 7mm (3/8in) wide sheer cream or pink ribbon.

Make the bead garland following the instructions for the garland (steps 1–4), making an 18cm (6in) length for each napkin ring. Coil the beaded wire to form a circle, then twist the ends together. To finish, tie short lengths of narrow sheer ribbon into the wire.

In a spin

BRINGING THE CHRISTMAS TREE INTO THE HOUSE IN THE MIDDLE OF DECEMBER IS SUCH AN EXCITING EVENT FOR CHILDREN AND ADULTS ALIKE. IT'S ALWAYS A DELIGHT TO GET THE OLD DECORATIONS OUT AND REMINISCE AS YOU HANG THEM ON THE TREE, BUT IT'S ALSO REFRESHING TO START ANEW OR JUST ADD ONE OR TWO NEW DECORATIONS EACH YEAR. THESE DELIGHTFUL BEAD TWISTS ARE SUCH AN UNUSUAL SHAPE THAT THEY'LL LOOK ABSOLUTELY STUNNING FOR BOTH TRADITIONAL AND CONTEMPORARY STYLED TREES. USE TINY DELICA BEADS TO MAKE THE BEAD TWISTS OR TRY PEARLS AND GIANT SILVER BEADS FOR THE BOLDER DESIGN DESCRIBED ON PAGE 47.

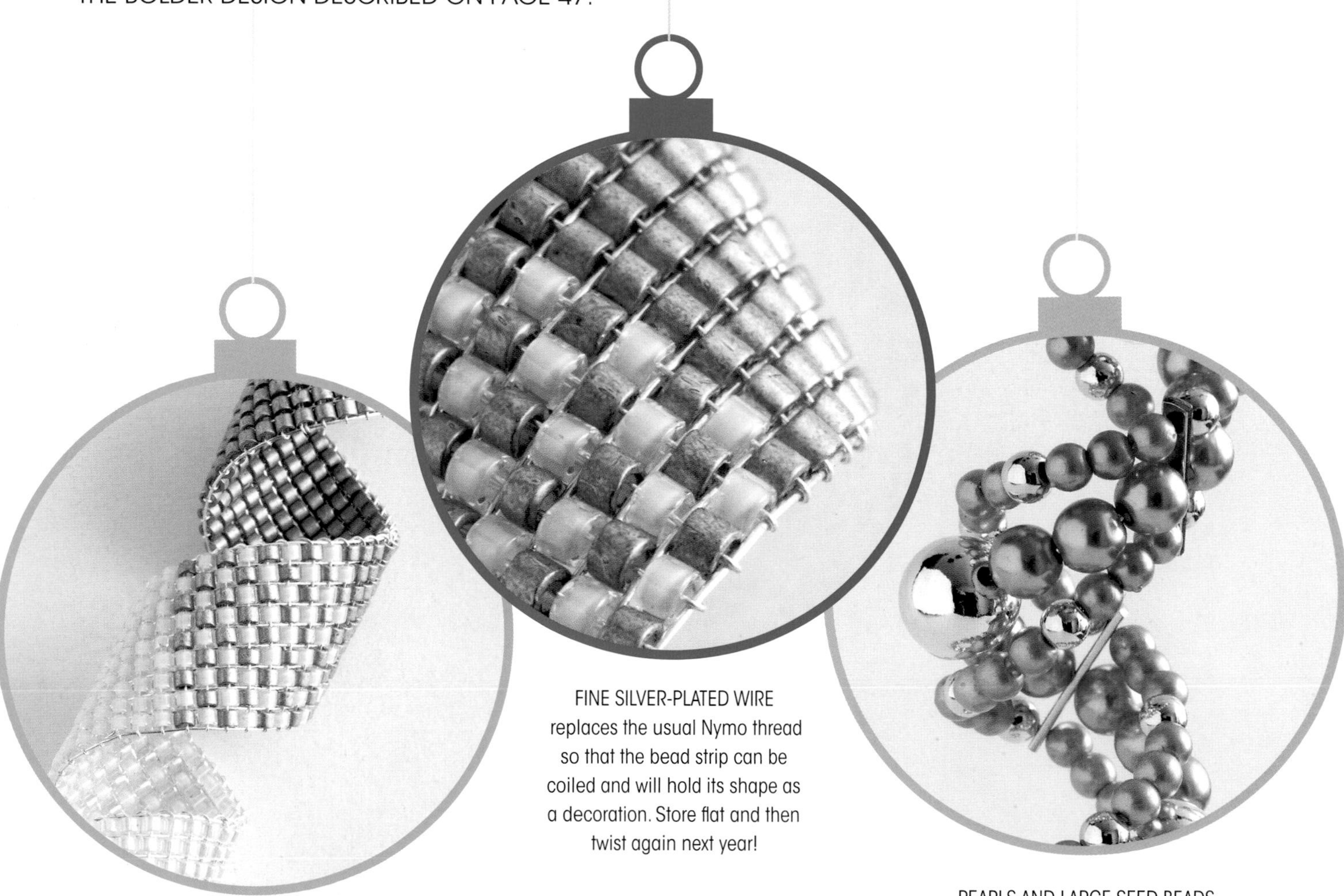

FINE SILVER-PLATED WIRE replaces the usual Nymo thread so that the bead strip can be coiled and will hold its shape as a decoration. Store flat and then twist again next year!

GRADUATE THE COLOURS of the beads so that there is a subtle change of shades along the length – with silver at one end, white at the other and pretty aqua in between.

PEARLS AND LARGE SEED BEADS strung on wire create a quick and easy decoration. Shiny silver beads that contrast with the subtle pearls really sparkle in the Christmas lights.

Bead twist decoration

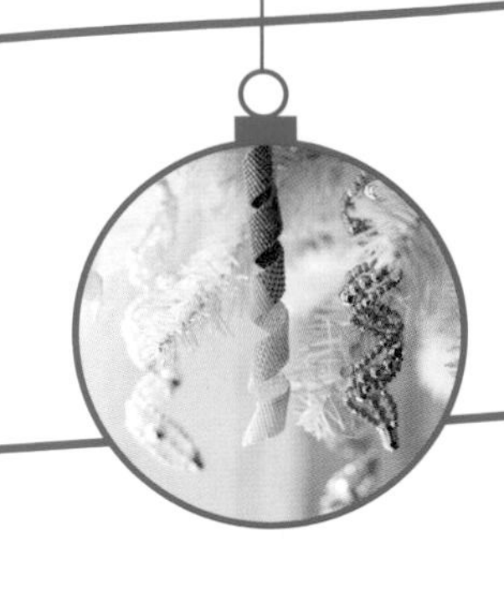

YOU WILL NEED (for one decoration)

- Antique or Delica beads 2g of white gold and 1g each of galvanized turquoise, galvanized satin-finish dark aqua, lined aqua mist AB, light aqua pearl, satin shimmering white AB, matte white
- Bead loom, 25cm (10in) long • Silver-plated wire, 0.315mm (30swg) and 0.2mm (36swg)
- Silver organza ribbon, 30cm (12in) x 2cm (¾in) wide

1 Set up the bead loom with eight 50cm (18in) lengths of 0.2mm silver-plated wire. Add the same length of 0.315mm wire on either side so that there are ten wires in all stretched across the loom (these wires are the warp threads). (See Techniques page 96 for bead loom basics.)

2 To add the weft thread, tie a 75cm (30in) length of 0.2mm wire to one of the thicker warp wires at one end of the loom to leave a 15cm (6in) tail. Pick up 9 white gold beads on the longer end. * Pass the weft wire under the warp threads and hold the beads in place with your finger so that one bead is between each pair of wires.

3 Feed the weft wire back through the beads so that the wire passes above the warp threads. Pull the weft wire tight. Pick up another 9 white gold beads and repeat from * until there are nine rows of beads.

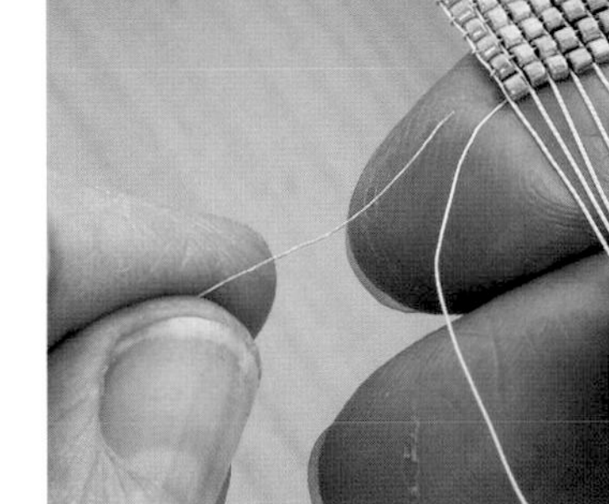

4 On the next row, to graduate the beads into the next colour, pick up alternate silver and galvanized turquoise beads to make 9 in all. Secure the beads as before and work another eight rows using mixed beads. Then work nine rows of just galvanized turquoise. Continue making the bead loom band, mixing the colours for nine rows and then working nine plain rows until you have added all seven colours.

5 To shape the end, add only 8 matte white beads in the next row, then 7 and so on until there is only a single bead. Turn the loom around and join on a length of 0.2mm silver-plated wire. Shape the end using white gold beads so that the white gold beads come to a point at the opposite side to the white beads.

6 Remove the bead panel from the loom. Feed each end of wire through the next row of beads and snip off close to the beadwork. Leave the thicker wire at the silver point until last. Pick up 15 white gold beads on the wire and feed the wire back through the bead at the point. Feed down through the next two rows and then cut off the tail.

7 Wrap the bead panel around a wooden spoon handle so that the spirals are close together. Pull out the handle and then pull the ends gently to open up the twists slightly. Tie the decoration on to the tree using a length of silver organza ribbon.

Fast 'n' festive

PEARL SPIRALS

This chunkier design can be made in any colours to suit your tree-decorating style. To make a pearl spiral you will need: ninety 4mm pearls, thirty 4mm silver beads, thirty 6mm pearls and five 10mm silver beads; four 3-hole bridges; two silver-plated tulip-end caps; 1m (1yd) of 0.7mm (22swg) silver-plated wire.

Cut three 30cm (12in) lengths of wire and twist together 2cm (¾in) from one end. On the middle wire, pick up 3 of the 6mm pearls, a 10mm silver bead and 3 more 6mm pearls. Feed the wire through the middle hole of a 3-hole bridge. On the outer wires pick up 3 of the 4mm pearls and a 4mm silver bead; repeat twice more. Feed the wires though the outer holes of the bridge. Repeat the same sequence between each bridge and then repeat the beads only. Twist the wires together at the other end, trim the two outer wires at both ends and feed the remaining wire through the tulip-end caps. Make a loop. Fold the loop flat at one end. Wrap the pearl decoration around a wooden spoon handle to create the twist and hang with gauze ribbon.

All lit up

IN THE NORTHERN PARTS OF THE WORLD CHRISTMAS COMES WHEN IT IS COLD OUTSIDE AND THE EVENINGS ARE LONG, SO WE NEED TO BRIGHTEN OUR HOMES AS MUCH AS POSSIBLE WITH PRETTY CANDLES AND LIGHTS TO CREATE A LOVELY WARM ATMOSPHERE. THESE BRIGHT, COLOURFUL POMPOM LIGHTS ARE IDEAL AND LOOK GORGEOUS EVEN WHEN UNLIT. THEY ARE A LITTLE TRICKY TO MAKE ALL IN ONE COLOUR BUT IF YOU USE SEVERAL COLOURS IT IS QUITE EASY TO FOLLOW THE SEQUENCE GIVEN IN THE BEADING DIAGRAM OVERLEAF AND THE POMPOMS COME TOGETHER IN NEXT TO NO TIME.

SILVER-LINED BEADS strung on fine wire and twisted around between the lights, disguises the electric cable and make the garland look much more attractive.

THE FROSTED FINISH on these inexpensive glass beads shows up as an attractive texture in the daylight and when lit makes the lights really sparkle.

ELASTIC THREAD is ideal for making the pompom lights as it makes it much easier to keep the beads tight as you work and the elasticity holds the ball of beads snugly around the light fitting.

Pompom lights

YOU WILL NEED (for one pompom)

• Frosted beads, thirty 10mm (eight pink, six lime, seven blue, four yellow and five orange) • Glass beads 8mm, five each of yellow, orange, pink, green and blue • Seed beads size 9 (2.5mm) 25g silver-lined crystal in mixed colours • Elastic thread 80cm (32in) of 0.5mm • Silver-plated wire 0.2mm (36swg) • White light garland with bulbs every 15cm (6in) • Sewing needle

1 Thread an 80cm (32in) length of elastic thread on to a sewing needle. Pick up 5 frosted pink beads and tie into a circle near one end of the elastic thread. Pass the needle back through the first bead. Pick up 4 lime beads and take the needle back through 2 pink beads (numbers 1 and 2 on the beading diagram below).

To make it easier to thread the elastic, pass a loop of sewing thread through the eye of the needle and then use the loop to pull the elastic thread back through.

2 Pick up 3 blue beads and take the needle back through the lime bead (6) and the next 2 pink beads (2 and 3). Pick up and add 3 yellow beads and go through blue (10) and 2 pinks (3 and 4), and then pick up and add 3 orange beads. Take the needle back through the yellow (13), 2 pinks (4 and 5) and a lime (9).

3 Finally, pick up 2 blue beads and pass the needle through the next orange (16), pink (5) and 2 limes (9 and 8). Pull the elastic tight to make a bowl shape, which forms the lower half of the pompom.

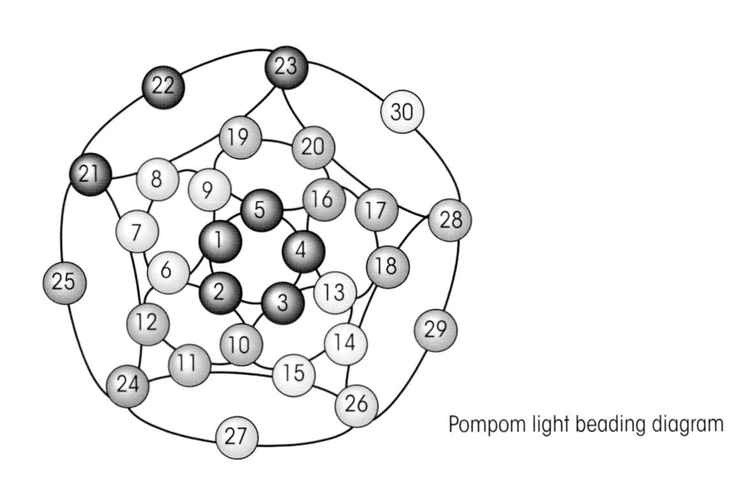

Pompom light beading diagram

4 Pick up 3 pink beads and take the needle back through the next blue (19), 2 limes (8 and 7) and blue (12). Pick up 2 orange beads and take the needle back through the next pink (21), lime (7), 2 blues (12 and 11) and yellow (15). Pick up 2 limes and pass the needle through the next orange (24), blue (11), 2 yellows (15 and 14) and orange (18).

5 Pick up 2 blues and take the needle back through the next lime (26), yellow (14), 3 orange (18, 17 and 16), blue (20) and pink (23). Finally, pick up the last bead, yellow and go through blue (28), 2 orange (17 and 16) and pink (5). You should now be back at the tail of elastic. Pull the elastic up as tightly as possible, tie the two tails together securely and then trim the ends. Make as many pompom lights as needed for your garland.

6 To decorate the electric cable, cut a 20cm (8in) length of silver-plated wire. Secure the wire to the top of the first light fitment by neatly twisting the wire round several times. Pick up 20 seed beads and an 8mm glass bead. Twist the large bead so that the wire twists and holds the bead securely next to the seed beads. Add 15 seed beads then another large bead and repeat until you've added all five colours. Pick up the last 20 seed beads, wrap the bead string around the electric cable and secure around the top of the next light fitment.

7 Decorate the electric cable between each of the light fitments in the same way. Now feed each bead pompom on to a light fitment through the ring of five pink beads so that they sit just above the ridge and are held securely.

If your light fitments don't have a ridge, wrap a small white elastic band several times around each light fitting and then push the bead pompom on to the fitment over the band.

GIVING AT CHRISTMAS

Ready for santa

WHO SAYS CHRISTMAS STOCKINGS ARE JUST FOR KIDS? INDULGE YOURSELF OR A FRIEND AND GET READY FOR SANTA BY MAKING THIS LUXURY DEVORÉ STOCKING TO HANG AS A DECORATION FROM THE MANTELPIECE OR FROM THE END OF THE BED – IF YOU'RE REALLY LUCKY IT WILL BE FULL OF SPECIAL LITTLE GIFTS ON CHRISTMAS MORNING! THE STOCKING IS MADE FROM SILK VELVET, WHICH CAN BE DYED ANY COLOUR YOU LIKE, OR SIMPLY LEAVE IT WHITE AND DECORATE WITH SPARKLING SILVER AND CRYSTAL BEADS FOR THE REALLY CLASSY LOOK SHOWN HERE. THERE IS ALSO AN EASY FELT VERSION OF THE STOCKING THAT CHILDREN WILL LOVE – SEE PAGE 59.

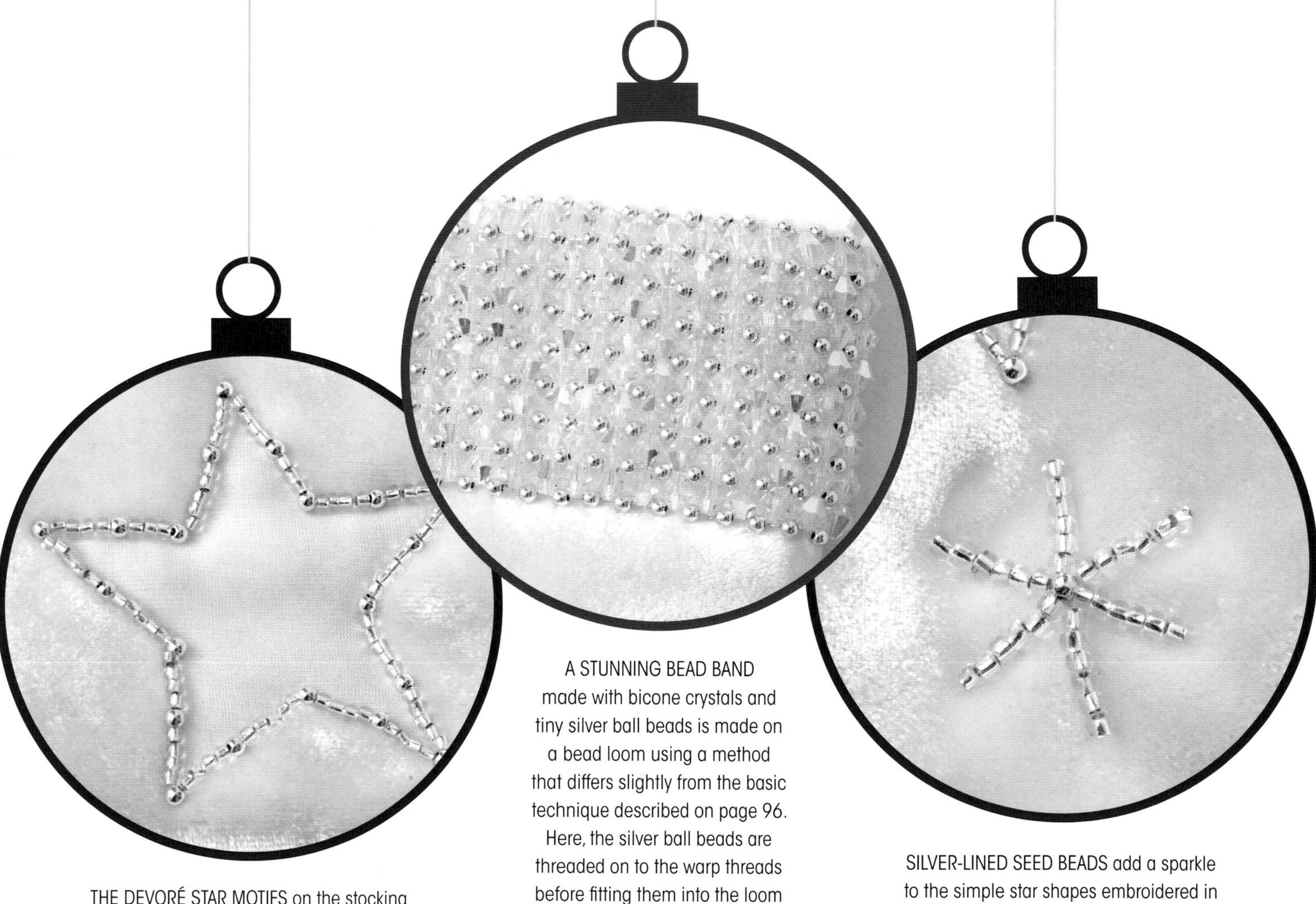

THE DEVORÉ STAR MOTIFS on the stocking are easy to create – simply paint Fibre Etch™ liquid on the reverse side of the velvet in a star shape, leave to dry and then iron. Like magic, the velvet pile washes away when wetted, leaving the star motifs.

A STUNNING BEAD BAND made with bicone crystals and tiny silver ball beads is made on a bead loom using a method that differs slightly from the basic technique described on page 96. Here, the silver ball beads are threaded on to the warp threads before fitting them into the loom and then the crystals are woven in using the weft thread as normal.

SILVER-LINED SEED BEADS add a sparkle to the simple star shapes embroidered in the gaps between the larger stars. Keep the beads at least 1cm (⅜in) from the tacked (basted) outline so that you can machine stitch the stocking easily.

Star stocking

YOU WILL NEED

• Fibre Etch™ • Silk velvet 56 x 38cm (22 x 15in) • Beading needle size 10 • Seed beads size 9 (2.5mm) 15g silver-lined clear • Bicone crystals (polished beads) 5mm, 200 • Silver ball beads 2.5mm, 300 • Bead loom 25cm (10in) long • Satin lining 75 x 38cm (30 x 15in) • Thin wadding 56 x 38cm (22 x 15in) • White sewing thread • Silver machine embroidery thread • Short length of cord

1 Enlarge the stocking template on page 103 to full size, trace on to tracing paper and cut out. Pin the stocking pattern on to the reverse side of a piece of silk velvet and draw around with a pencil. Trace a star on to thin card and cut out. Using the template as a guide, draw around the card star four times on to the stocking shape. Following the manufacturer's guidelines, apply the Fibre Etch straight from the bottle on to the star shapes. Keep within the lines and make sure each star is completely wetted with Fibre Etch. Dry with a hair dryer.

2 Press the reverse side of the stocking shape with a medium dry iron until the star shapes start to turn slightly brown. Keep checking until the colour changes and the fabric feels brittle. Rinse out under a cold running tap, rubbing the pile away with your fingers. Hang until almost dry and then press on the reverse side.

Although it is easy to use, if you haven't tried Fibre Etch before, draw the star shape on to a scrap of velvet and try it out so that you know exactly what to expect on the real stocking.

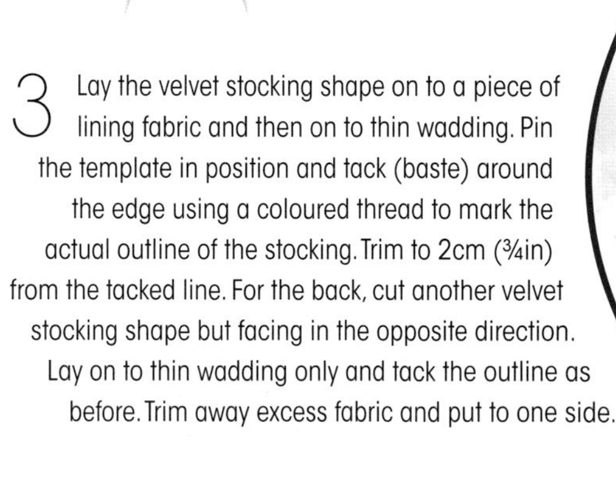

3 Lay the velvet stocking shape on to a piece of lining fabric and then on to thin wadding. Pin the template in position and tack (baste) around the edge using a coloured thread to mark the actual outline of the stocking. Trim to 2cm (¾in) from the tacked line. For the back, cut another velvet stocking shape but facing in the opposite direction. Lay on to thin wadding only and tack the outline as before. Trim away excess fabric and put to one side.

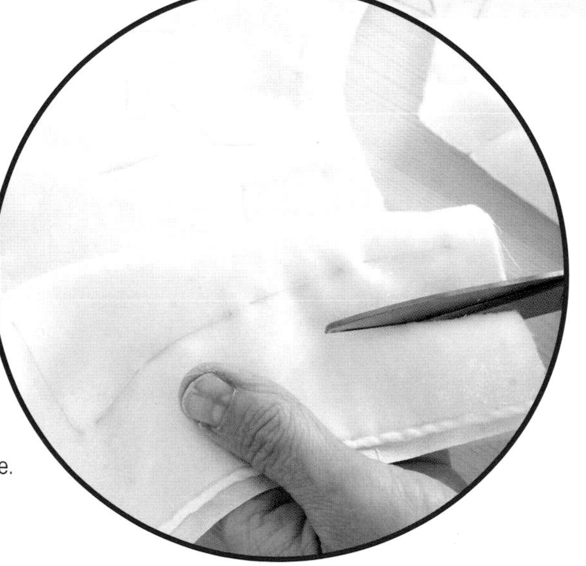

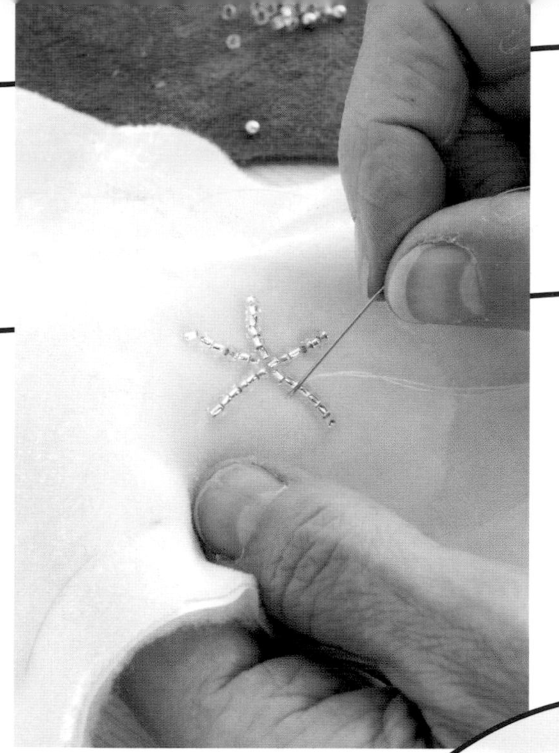

4 Secure a double length of sewing thread on the reverse side of the stocking panel and bring out between the stars. Pick up 6 silver-lined seed beads and take the needle back through the fabric so the beads are in a straight line. Couch over the beads in the middle (see page 99 for couching). Sew five more 'legs' to make a simple star shape and then sew a silver ball bead in the middle.

To prevent beads falling off in use and for extra strength, always use a double thread to attach beads and secure the threads on the reverse side with a double backstitch.

5 Bring a double thread out at the point of an etched star shape, pick up a silver ball bead and 4 silver-lined seed beads twice, then a final silver ball bead. Take the needle back through at the V shape of the star and then, using the same needle, couch over the bead strand several times to secure it. Repeat the process on each side of the star, altering the number of seed beads to suit until the star is complete. Add beads to each star in the same way.

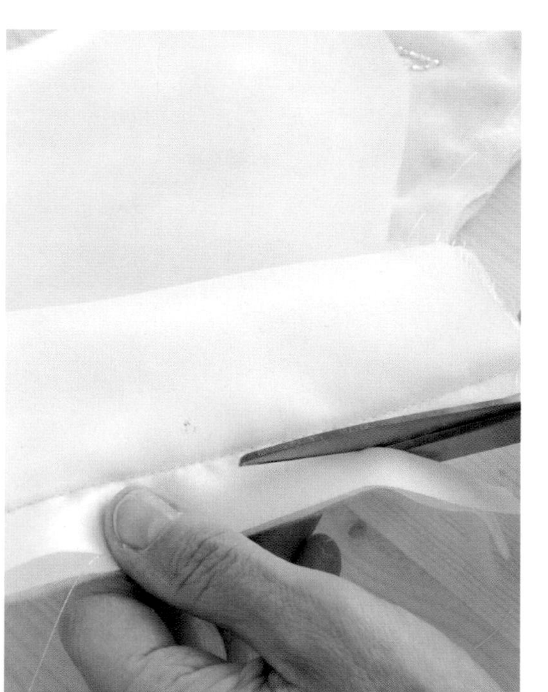

6 Fold the lining fabric with right sides together and cut two stocking shapes using the template and adding a 2cm (¾in) seam allowance all round. Pin a lining stocking with right sides together to each of the prepared velvet stocking panels. Sew along the top straight edge, trim to 6mm (¼in) and press open.

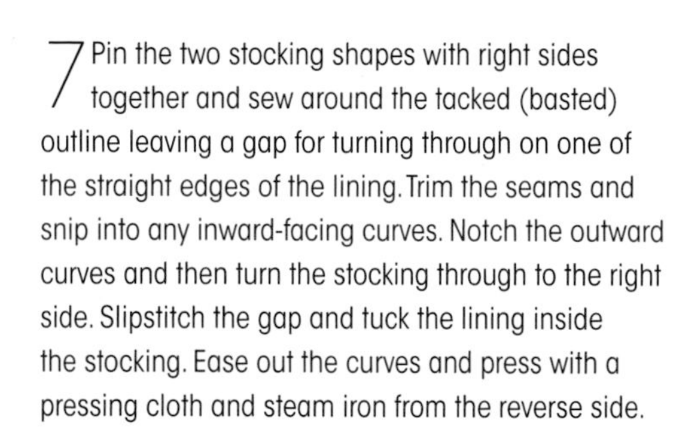

7 Pin the two stocking shapes with right sides together and sew around the tacked (basted) outline leaving a gap for turning through on one of the straight edges of the lining. Trim the seams and snip into any inward-facing curves. Notch the outward curves and then turn the stocking through to the right side. Slipstitch the gap and tuck the lining inside the stocking. Ease out the curves and press with a pressing cloth and steam iron from the reverse side.

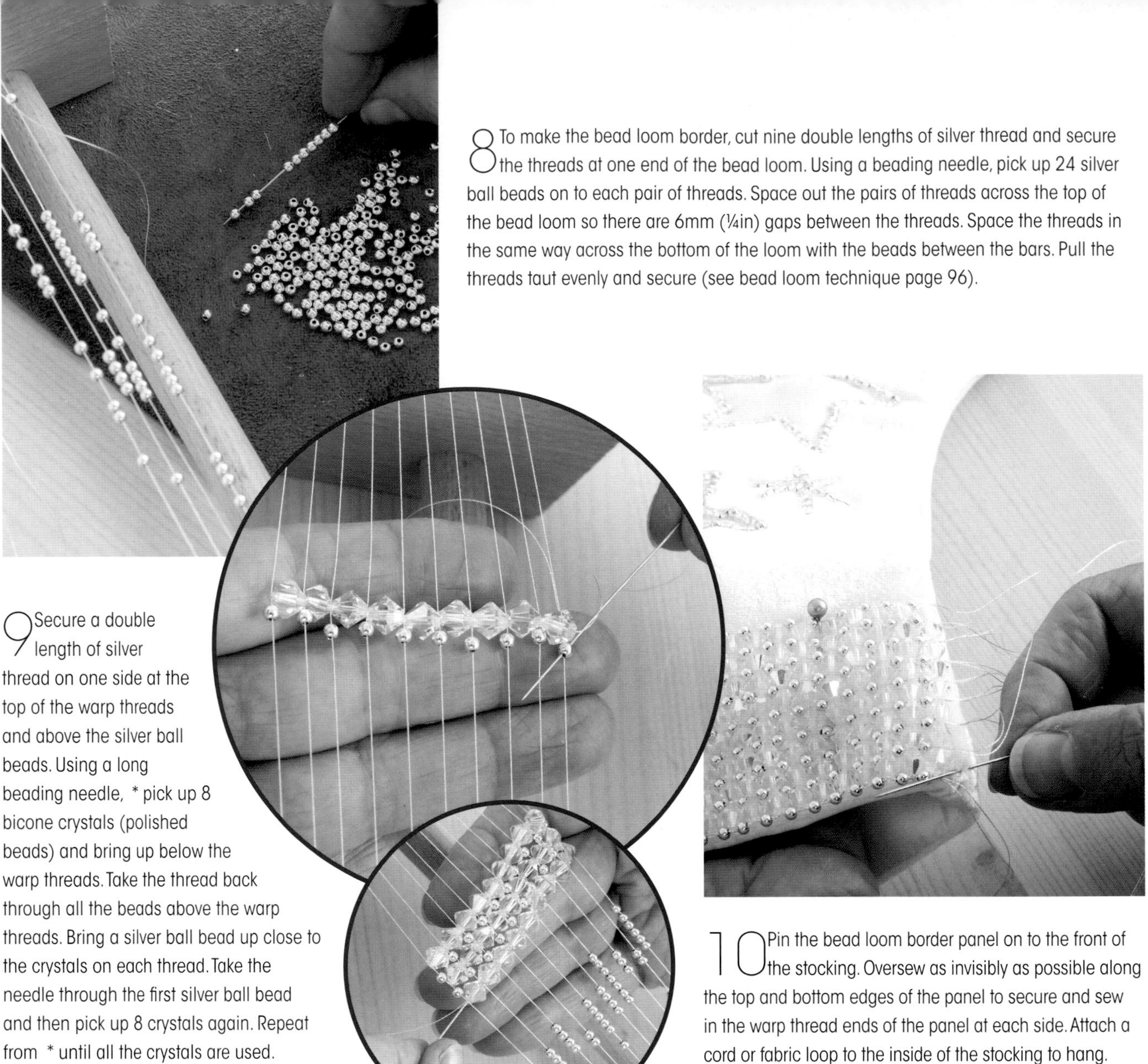

8 To make the bead loom border, cut nine double lengths of silver thread and secure the threads at one end of the bead loom. Using a beading needle, pick up 24 silver ball beads on to each pair of threads. Space out the pairs of threads across the top of the bead loom so there are 6mm (¼in) gaps between the threads. Space the threads in the same way across the bottom of the loom with the beads between the bars. Pull the threads taut evenly and secure (see bead loom technique page 96).

9 Secure a double length of silver thread on one side at the top of the warp threads and above the silver ball beads. Using a long beading needle, * pick up 8 bicone crystals (polished beads) and bring up below the warp threads. Take the thread back through all the beads above the warp threads. Bring a silver ball bead up close to the crystals on each thread. Take the needle through the first silver ball bead and then pick up 8 crystals again. Repeat from * until all the crystals are used.

10 Pin the bead loom border panel on to the front of the stocking. Oversew as invisibly as possible along the top and bottom edges of the panel to secure and sew in the warp thread ends of the panel at each side. Attach a cord or fabric loop to the inside of the stocking to hang.

Ring the changes

PIXIE STOCKING

This stocking is quicker to make than the devoré one as there is no lining. You will need: two 22 x 32cm (8½ x 12½in) pieces of purple felt; small pieces of lime, orange, pink and turquoise felt; seed beads in lime, orange, pink and turquoise; decorative bells, six each in lime, orange, pink, turquoise and purple; silver-plated jump rings, purple sewing thread; beading needle.

Enlarge and trace the stocking template from page 103 and pin on to two layers of purple felt and cut out with a 6mm (¼in) seam allowance. Cut out a star in each of the other felt colours and pin on to one stocking. Couch matching seed beads around the stars, catching the felt down as you go. Add a single bead at each point and stitch through a single bead in the centre of the star several times. Stitch the two stockings together around the edge using matching thread. Cut a triangle 3.2cm (1¼in) wide x 5.5cm (2⅛in) long from each of the felt colours (not purple), to fit along the stocking top. Pick up a turquoise bell on a jump ring and close the ring (see page 102). Pick up a second turquoise bell on another jump ring, then loop on the first bell by its jump ring and finally a third bell. Feed the jump ring through the seed bead in the centre of the turquoise star and close it up. Make a different cluster of bells for each of the stars and another four clusters for the felt triangles. Add a third jump ring to the top of each of these clusters and sew that jump ring to the back of the matching felt triangles.

Sew the triangles along the top of the stocking and couch beads along the line, changing the colours to suit the felt. Finally, add a loop of ribbon for hanging and a few purple bells to the back edge.

Poinsettia perfection

DON'T YOU JUST LOVE WHEN POINSETTIAS APPEAR IN SHOPS IN DECEMBER? THEY HAVE A WONDERFUL SHAPE THAT IS INSTANTLY RECOGNISABLE – HUGE BRIGHT RED OR OFF-WHITE BLOOMS CONTRASTING WITH ABUNDANT DEEP GREEN LEAVES. THEY IMPART A CHRISTMAS MOOD INSTANTLY, WHICH MAKES THEM THE IDEAL EMBELLISHMENT FOR A CHRISTMAS PARTY BAG. USE BRIGHT RED SILK WITH DEEP RED AND FUCHSIA BEADS FOR A RICH, CLASSIC LOOK OR WHITE AND CRYSTAL FOR A WINTER WEDDING.

THE SILK DUPION BRACTS are painted with Decoform™ a stiffening liquid, which holds the shape once it has dried and also helps prevent the fabric fraying.

USE FUCHSIA BEADS AND WIRE alongside the red beads and wire to really lift the design. The colour change is very subtle but adds further interest to the flower centre.

WHITE AND CRYSTAL BEADS and silver-plated wire make a pristine white poinsettia really sparkle, while different sized beads make the flower centre the focal point (see page 63).

Red poinsettia

YOU WILL NEED

• Red silk dupion two 20cm (8in) squares • Red silk organza 20cm (8in) square • Red tulle 20cm (8in) square • Bonding web 20cm (8in) square • Red and fuchsia craft wire, 0.5mm (25swg) • Red bugles 5g each of 20mm (¾in), 12mm (½in) and 6mm (¼in) • Red beads, about eight each of 3 x 9mm teardrops, 4mm crystals, 3 x 4mm droplets, pony beads and seed beads • Fuchsia crystals, eight 4mm • Decoform™

1 Iron the bonding web on to one of the silk squares, peel off the backing paper and lay the other silk square on top. Press with a medium-hot iron to fuse the layers together. Trace the two poinsettia templates from page 106 on to white paper and cut out, cutting along the petal lines towards the centre. Lay the larger template on to the silk square and draw around the edge with a pencil. Fold back every alternate bract (petal) and extend the lines into the centre. Cut out the bracts individually.

2 Cut seven 20cm (8in) lengths of red craft wire. Twist a loop at one end and pick up a 6mm bugle and 5 of the 12mm bugles. Lay the wire down the centre of the first bract so that the short bugle is near the tip. Using matching sewing thread, oversew a couple of stitches across the wire at the bottom end of the bract. Work up the wire, oversewing two stitches between each bugle. Oversew above the last bugle then trim the wire to 6mm (¼in) above the bract and bend the tip over to the reverse side. Sew a few stitches to secure and trim neatly. Repeat for the other six bracts. Now paint the backs of the petals with the Decoform liquid and bend the petals into attractive shapes and allow to dry.

3 Pin the smaller template on to the tulle and organza squares and cut around the edge, cutting in towards the centre as indicated by the lines on the template. Fold the poinsettia-shaped pieces in four to find the centre and then cut a tiny hole through both layers.

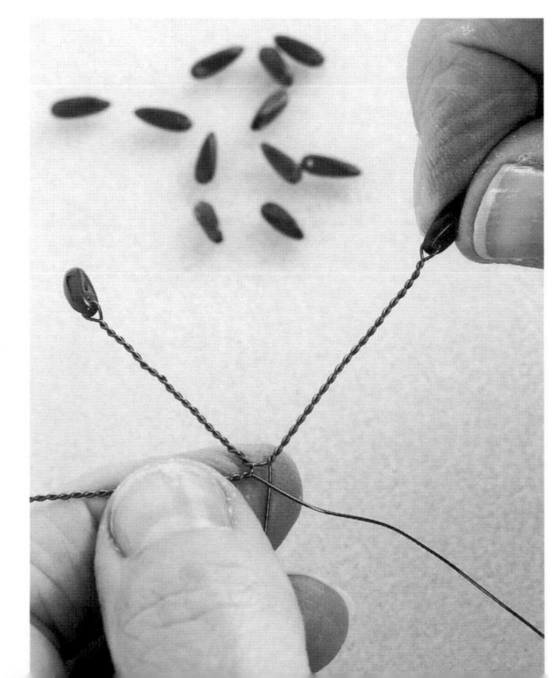

4 Cut a length of red craft wire. Pick up a red teardrop and fold the wire over about 8cm (3in) from the end. Twist the teardrop until the wire is tightly twisted for about 3cm (1¼in). Pick up another teardrop and twist the wire to make another slightly different length stem. Repeat to make seven stems in all.

5 Make similar groups of wired beads using small red droplets and use fuchsia wire to create groups of wired fuchsia crystals, Hold all three groups of wired beads together and twist to secure into a mini bouquet for the centre of the poinsettia. Make another set of wired beads with 4cm (1½in) long stems using the fuchsia crystals and put to one side.

6 Pick up a 20mm (¾in) red bugle on red craft wire and then a pony bead and a seed bead. Take the wire back through the pony bead and bugle. Using the long tail, make another six bugle-beaded wires. Tuck the mini bouquet into the centre of tulle poinsettia. Hold the fabric up around the beads and wrap one of the wires around the base to secure. Wrap the bugle stems around the poinsettia and then feed the organza over the wires. Wrap the long fuchsia-beaded wires around the organza and wrap with a wire end to secure.

7 Arrange the bracts around the poinsettia centre and wrap one of the wires tightly around the base to secure. Open out the bracts and shape them by bending the bugle-covered wire. Fold the wires to make a thicker stem. Wrap the wires using floral tape. Attach a brooch back or hatpin to the poinsettia and pin to a bag, hat or garment.

Ring the changes

WHITE POINSETTIA

If red is not your colour why not make a pristine white poinsettia instead? These flowers are very versatile – use as a corsage or bag embellishment for a winter wedding or festive ball, or make several to decorate the tree or to make your Christmas table look fabulous. Attach them to plain napkin rings or arrange around a selection of candles for a really eye-catching display.

Use the same materials list and instructions as the red poinsettia but change the fabrics to white, the beads, crystals and bugles to white or clear and the wire to silver-plated wire.

Festive greetings

CHRISTMAS COMES BUT ONCE A YEAR SO WHY ARE WE ALWAYS SENDING CARDS AT THE LAST MINUTE? THESE GORGEOUS CARDS ARE SURELY THE IDEAL WAY TO GET AHEAD AS THEY ARE SO QUICK AND EASY TO MAKE AND THE STYLISH, CONTEMPORARY DESIGNS WILL DELIGHT WHOEVER RECEIVES THEM. THE SISAL SHAPES ARE REALLY UNUSUAL AND LOOK WONDERFUL WITH A BEAD AND WIRE EMBELLISHMENT. LOOK FOR REALLY CLASSY CHRISTMAS PAPERS IN BRIGHT RASPBERRY REDS AND LIME GREENS TO MAKE THE CARD AND COMPLETE THE DESIGNS WITH PRETTY POLKA DOT RIBBON, RICKRACK BRAID AND BIG SPOTTY BRADS.

WRAP WIRE, which has been threaded with a selection of beads, around the bottom of a piece of decorated card to make a simple tag. If you make the tag from a folded card all the rough edges can be hidden inside.

SISAL SHAPES have a wonderful rough texture that contrasts with the shiny beads and wire. There are lots of different Christmas designs to choose from such as stars, snowflakes, hearts and even reindeer.

SORT PRETTY, STAR-SHAPED BEADS into colour ranges, such as pinks and reds or greens to create greater impact on card designs and choose paper, ribbons and embellishments to match.

Star card

YOU WILL NEED

• Two sisal stars • Star beads in red, pink and clear, about four of each • Mixed beads in red and clear, about twenty • Seed beads, size 11 (2mm), 5g red • Silver-plated wire, 1m (1yd) of 0.4mm (27swg) • Textured off-white card A4 (American letter) • Christmas stripe paper • Polka dot ribbon, 25cm (10in) x 2cm (¾in) wide • Craft glue dots • Round-nosed pliers

1 Cut a 40cm (16in) length of silver-plated wire and make a loop at one end to stop the beads falling off. * Pick up a red seed bead, a larger bead and another red seed bead; then pick up a star bead. Repeat from *, changing the colour of the star bead from red, to pink and then clear, until there are about 7 star beads on the wire.

2 Wind the wire around a pair of round-nosed pliers to make a loop near the plain end. Bring the first three beads down to the loop and then make a second loop at the other side of the beads. Bring a star bead down the wire and make a loop at the other side. Continue making loops to one side or the other to space the beads along the length of the wire. Move some of the seed beads into the loops.

3 Cut an 18 x 13cm (7 x 5in) piece of off-white cream card. Score across the middle and fold in half to make a landscape-shaped card. Cut a piece of stripe paper to fit the front and tear down one long side about 2.5cm (1in) from the edge. Stick the paper on the front of the card so that the long straight side is across the bottom edge.

If you tear the paper towards you, the white core of the paper makes an attractive edge; if you tear it away from you there is no white edge.

4 Stick a length of polka dot ribbon across the paper and trim neatly. Attach a sisal star using a glue dot.

5 Arrange the beaded wire across the card and bend to make an attractive arrangement. Use glue dots behind some of the star beads to attach the beaded wire. Attach a few single star beads on the right-hand side.

Fast 'n' festive

TAGS

Cut a 6 x 21cm (2⅜ x 8¼in) piece of off-white textured card. Score across the middle and fold in half to make a tall landscape-shaped tag. Stick striped paper and a sisal star on the front. Wrap wire around the tag, adding beads across the front. For the green tag, cut a piece of green vellum to fit the front of the tag and tear off the bottom edge. Stick on the tag with double-sided tape down the centre only. Stick polka dot ribbon down the middle and trim at an angle. Wrap wire around the snowflake, adding beads across the front only. Finish both tags with polka dot ribbon, rickrack braid and a large polka dot brad.

Ring the changes

SNOWFLAKE CARD

Why not send wishes of a white Christmas with this sparkling snowflake card? This attractive lime green greeting can be made with or without the beaded wire decoration. Simply cut a 21 x 16.5cm (8¼ x 6½in) piece of off-white textured card. Score across the middle and fold in half. Cut a piece of striped paper to fit half the card and stick on the front. Tear a piece of green vellum and stick next to the striped paper. Cover the join with polka dot ribbon and attach the snowflake. Finish by attaching a green bead and wire decoration.

Bags of gifts

GIFT BAGS ARE IDEAL FOR REALLY TINY PRESENTS THAT ARE DIFFICULT TO WRAP – SIMPLY WRAP THE GIFT IN TONING TISSUE PAPER AND POP IT INSIDE THE BAG. EACH OF THE BAGS SHOWN HERE ARE MADE IN THE SAME WAY FROM WIDE WIRE-EDGED RIBBON SO THERE ARE NO AWKWARD SEAMS TO FINISH. HAVE FUN USING UP YOUR LEFTOVER BEADS BY VARYING THE BEADS AND THE DESIGN OF THE FRINGING. THE GIFT BAGS SHOWN ON PAGE 71 GIVE AN IDEA OF HOW EVERY BAG CAN BE MADE AS UNIQUE AS THE GIFTS INSIDE, SIMPLY BY CHANGING THE BEAD COLOUR AND PATTERN, .

LARGER BEADS are only added at the end of alternate strands of a plain bead fringe with strands in between slightly shorter so that the fringe has weight but still hangs straight. Repeat bead patterns on alternate strands to co-ordinate the design.

SHORT BUGLES AND BRIGHT PINK PEARLS add a contrast of textures to this simple looped fringe. Begin by securing the thread at one side and make the small loops first. Work back across adding the longer loops then attach a few bead loops to the neck of the gift bag.

ATTACH A FEW BEAD STRANDS to a short length of craft wire and secure around the neck of the gift bag before tying the ribbon bow. The bead strands add a finishing touch, making the beads the focal point.

Ribbon gift bag

YOU WILL NEED (for the raspberry bag)

- Sheer raspberry wire-edged ribbon, 38cm (15in) x 7cm (2¾in) wide and 50cm (20in) x 2.5cm (1in) wide
- Raspberry and lime sewing thread • Seed beads size 11 (2mm), 2g each of lime and bright green
- Crystals 5mm, twenty green • Teardrop beads 3 x 10mm, thirteen green • Beading needle size 10
- Silver-plated craft wire 10cm (4in) of 0.5mm (25swg)

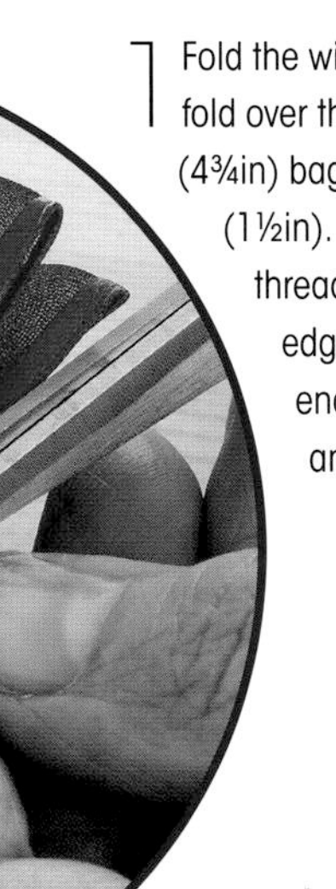

1 Fold the wider sheer ribbon in half and then fold over the ends to the inside to make a 12cm (4¾in) bag shape. Trim the folded ends to 4cm (1½in). Sew the side seams with matching thread beginning 3cm (1¼in) from the top edge. Reverse for a few stitches at each end of the seam to secure the threads and then trim neatly.

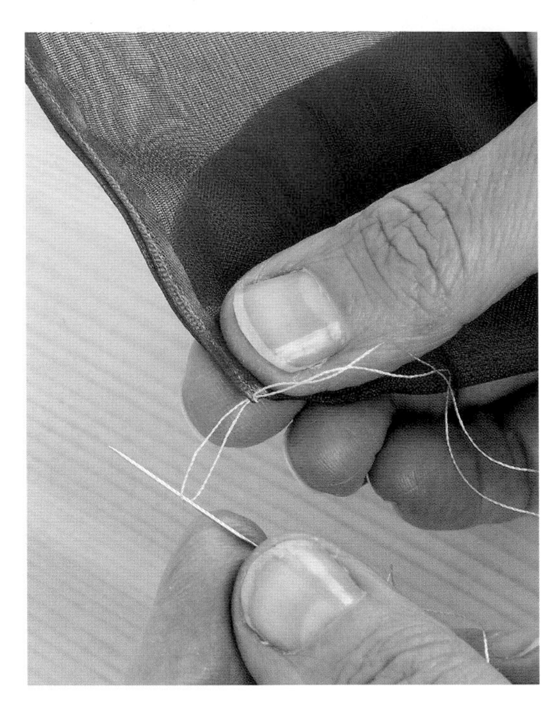

If your ribbon is a slightly different width simply insert pins along the bottom edge to divide into seven equal spaces.

2 To begin the bead fringe, cut eight 30cm (12in) lengths of lime sewing thread. Fold a length in half and feed the cut ends into the beading needle. Sew a tiny stitch into the corner of the bag and then take the needle through the loop and pull taut. Add a double thread in the same way at 1cm (⅜in) gaps and into the other corner. Leave the needle on the last pair of threads.

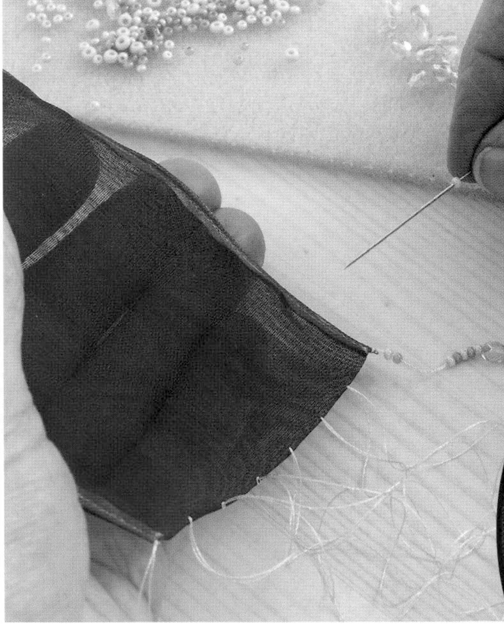

3 Using the threaded needle, pick up 7 seed beads, alternating between lime and bright green, then pick up a crystal, a further 6 seed beads and another crystal. Leave the pair of thread ends lying.

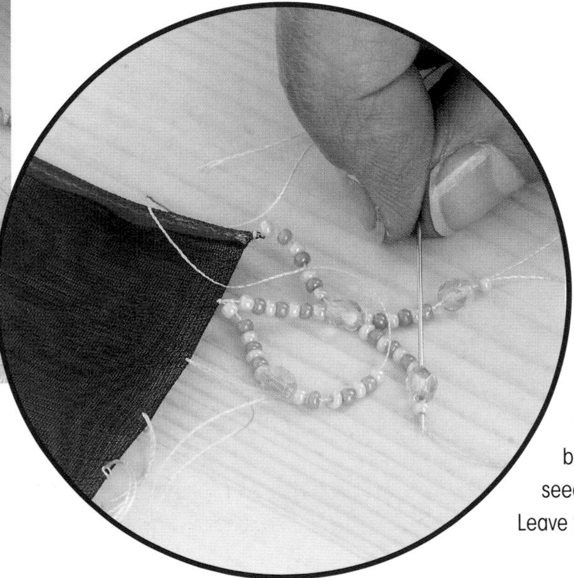

4 Thread the beading needle with one of the threads from the next pair. Pick up 7 seed beads, alternating between lime and bright green, and then take the needle through the first crystal on the adjacent bead strand. Add a further 6 seed beads and another crystal. Leave the thread end lying.

5 Thread the beading needle on to the other single thread and pick up 7 seed beads, a crystal, 7 seed beads and feed the needle through the last crystal on the adjacent bead strand. Leave the thread lying. Repeat steps 4 and 5 to bead each pair of threads across the bottom of the bag. Finish the bead fringing by threading the final pair of threads at the other corner on to a needle and picking up the same sequence of beads as the opposite corner.

For an added surprise, sprinkle a few drops of scented oil on to the tissue paper before wrapping the gift.

6 On each pair of threads along the bottom of the fringing pick up a seed bead and a teardrop bead. Feed the needle back through the seed bead and then up through the bead strand. Work a half hitch knot (see diagram on page 100) on either side of the top crystal and then feed the thread through a few more seed beads before trimming the end.

7 Attach a long double length of thread on to the wire by feeding the needle through the loop and pulling taut. Pick up the beads listed in step 3 to make a single-beaded strand. Take the needle back through the seed beads and crystals. Work a half hitch over the wire and then make another similar strand a slightly different length. Make five bead strands in all and secure the thread. Fill the gift bag, secure with the beaded wire and then tie the narrow sheer ribbon in a bow. Trim the ends neatly to finish.

I'ts party time!

CHRISTMAS IS THE PRIME TIME OF YEAR FOR PARTIES SO THERE IS ALWAYS AN EXCUSE TO DRESS UP. THE SIMPLEST PARTY FROCK WILL LOOK SIMPLY STUNNING WHEN YOU TEAM IT WITH THIS SCRUMPTIOUS SET OF NECKLACE AND EARRINGS (SEE PAGE 76). THE RICH BERRY COLOURS OF THE BEADS SPARKLE AGAINST THE PRETTY GOLD CHAIN AND THE SHEER RIBBON ADDS A CONTEMPORARY TOUCH, SOFTENING THE EFFECT AND MAKING IT PERFECT FOR THE FESTIVE SEASON. MAKE A PRETTY BRACELET AS WELL (SEE PAGE 77 FOR INSTRUCTIONS), TO WEAR ON ITS OWN OR MATCH WITH THE NECKLACE AND EARRINGS. CHOOSE A FAIRLY LARGE GOLD CHAIN SO THE RIBBON WEAVES THROUGH THE LINKS EASILY.

SHEER BURGUNDY RIBBON looks absolutely fabulous against pale skin at Christmas time. If these rich, warm tones are not your favourite, change to white, champagne and crystal instead.

MAKE BEAD CHARMS from a selection of pretty beads in warm, rich tones to attach to the necklace. For a larger embellishment in the centre of the necklace attach charms to a short length of chain.

LUXURY FASTENINGS are essential when you make an extra special piece of jewellery, especially if you have short hair or plan to wear your hair up! A good quality heavyweight design sets off the wide burgundy ribbon.

Beaded bow necklace

YOU WILL NEED

• Mixed beads in dark raspberry, deep burgundy and black • Washer-style and tubular gold-finish beads, twenty each • Large multicolour pebble beads 15mm, four • Gold-plated wire 0.6mm (24swg) • Gold headpins, twenty • Gold-plated chain with 5mm links 30cm (12in) • Gold-plated jump ring • Necklace fastening with gold finish • Sheer burgundy ribbon, 0.5m (½yd) x 1.5cm (⅝in) wide and 60cm (24in) x 3.5cm (1⅜in) wide

1 Pick up 2 small beads on gold-plated wire straight off the reel, then add a large pebble bead and 2 more small beads. Use round-nosed pliers to make an eyepin loop on the end of the wire (see Techniques page 101).

2 Drop the beads down to the eyepin loop and then make another loop at the other side of the beads. Trim the wire close to where it crosses over and then straighten the loops (see Techniques page 101). Make four links altogether with a large pebble bead in the middle and slightly different beads at either side each time.

3 Cut six lengths of gold chain with five links in each piece. Lay the bead links out with a piece of chain at each end and one in between each link. Open the ends of the bead links and attach the chains to make the necklace. Use a small gold jump ring to attach the remaining piece of chain to the centre link in the middle of the necklace.

Use wire cutters and snip into both sides of the sixth link along, so that it falls away to leave a five-link chain.

4 To make the bead charms pick up a large bead on a gold headpin and then 1 or 2 small beads. Trim the end of the headpin to 7mm (⅜in). Bend the headpin to one side with snipe-nosed pliers and then use the round-nosed pliers to bend the wire into a ring (see Techniques page 101). Make twenty-three different charms, keeping them all fairly short.

5 Open the ring on four of the charms and attach them one at a time into the same centre link on one of the plain chain lengths. Attach four more charms to each centre link. Attach a single charm to each of the links on the dangling chain in the centre of the necklace and one into the jump ring at the top.

6 Make or buy two thong ends in gold wire. To make a thong end, wind gold wire around a crochet hook or knitting needle about seven times to make a tight spring. Take the spring off and trim the ends. Use the snipe-nosed pliers to open out one ring at one end.

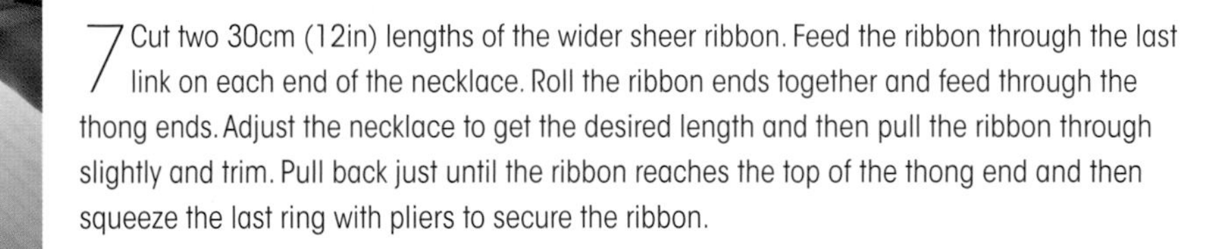

7 Cut two 30cm (12in) lengths of the wider sheer ribbon. Feed the ribbon through the last link on each end of the necklace. Roll the ribbon ends together and feed through the thong ends. Adjust the necklace to get the desired length and then pull the ribbon through slightly and trim. Pull back just until the ribbon reaches the top of the thong end and then squeeze the last ring with pliers to secure the ribbon.

8 Lay the necklace down and arrange the chain so that it is untwisted and position the charms as you would like them to hang. Cut five 10cm (4in) lengths of the narrower ribbon and feed one through the centre link on each piece of chain. Tie in a simple knot and then trim the ends of the ribbons at an angle.

9 Open the rings at the end of the necklace and attach an attractive gold toggle fastening or other ornate necklace fastening. Alternatively, for a really dramatic look you could tie the necklace ends together with ribbon and let the ends drape down your back.

BEADED BOW EARRINGS

Make a quick pair of earrings to match the necklace. You will need: two pebble beads; four smaller beads; two five-link lengths of gold-plated chain; two earring wires; some narrow sheer ribbon.

Make a large charm with the pebble bead at the bottom and one or two small beads on top, as in step 1 page 74. Attach the charm to a five-link length of gold-plated chain. Attach an earring wire to the top of the chain and then tie a length of sheer ribbon through the bottom link of the chain and trim diagonally.

For an alternative look, simply substitute the gold chain for a silver chain. Use blue beads for a cool contemporary feel.

Ribbon chain bracelet

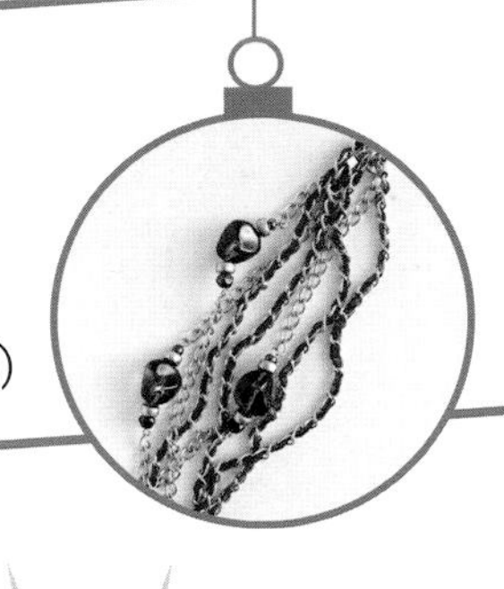

YOU WILL NEED

• Gold-plated chain with 5mm links 1.25m (1½yd) • Sheer burgundy ribbon, 1m (40in) x 6mm (¼in) wide • Pebble beads 15mm, three • Medium-sized mixed beads, ten–twelve • Gold washer-style beads, seven • Gold tube bead, two • Gold-plated wire 0.6mm (24swg) • Large gold tube crimp 3mm (⅛in), ten • Gold-plated jump rings 5mm (¼in) sixteen • Toggle fastening rings 7mm (⅜in), two • Toggle fastening 12mm (½in)

1 Cut five 15cm (6in) lengths of gold-plated chain. Bend a 10cm (4in) piece of scrap wire in half and twist one end tightly to make a 'needle'. Thread a 25cm (10in) length of ribbon on to the needle and weave it through the chain links on one length. Thread ribbon through all the lengths.

If the chain you buy has links larger than 5mm, simply buy wider ribbon to get the same effect.

2 Thread the ribbon through a large tube crimp and then a jump ring and back through the crimp. Thread it through the last link in the chain and back through the crimp. Pull the ribbon with both ends to manoeuvre the chain, crimp and jump rings close together. Trim the ribbon tail and then squeeze the crimp to flatten and secure the ribbon. Repeat at both ends of all the chains.

The small toggle rings are part of a bracelet fastening but the bar section is not required for this design and can be put aside.

3 Make three bead links using the large pebble beads following steps 1 and 2 on page 74. Cut three pieces of chain 13cm (5in) long. Cut one in half and cut the other two 4cm (1½in) from one end. Attach a link between the cut pieces of chain. Arrange the beads lengths between the ribbon chains so that the beads step down the bracelet. Attach the chains to the small toggle ring with jump rings. Repeat at the other end. Attach a bracelet toggle fastening to each of the smaller toggle rings. Make four bead charms and attach to the end of a five-link chain. To finish, attach the chain to the jump ring at the large round toggle fastening.

Christmas wishes

EVEN IF TIME IS SHORT IN THE RUN UP TO CHRISTMAS IT IS ALWAYS WORTH MAKING AN EFFORT TO CREATE SOME REALLY SPECIAL CARDS FOR A FEW CLOSE FRIENDS OR FAMILY MEMBERS. THESE BRIGHTLY COLOURED FESTIVE CARDS ARE IDEAL AS THEY ARE FAIRLY QUICK TO MAKE AND THE DELIGHTFUL POP-OUT TECHNIQUE MAKES THEM LOOK QUITE SPECTACULAR. THE CARDS ARE MADE PRIMARILY USING SHINY ACCENT BEADS, WHICH ARE TINY NO-HOLE BEADS THAT ARE SIMPLY SPRINKLED ON TO A VERY STICKY TAPE. THE INSTRUCTIONS OVERLEAF DESCRIBE THE CHRISTMAS TREE CARD – SEE PAGE 81 FOR THE OTHER TWO CARDS.

DECORATING WITH ACCENT BEADS is easy but it is essential to begin with the largest beads, such as seed beads and bugles, and work down to the accent beads, with the tiny accent beads used last to fill in any small nooks and crannies.

CREATING DESIGN DETAILS within a beaded background, such as the snowman's face and the scarf fringe, is straightforward – just remember to add the features first and then fill in with the background beads, starting with seed beads and working down to the accent beads.

EXTRA BEAD DETAILS, like the holly 'berries' on the Christmas pudding can be added at the end using strong glue or a multi-surface paint such as Pébéo Touch. For best results choose paint the same colour as the beads or glue that dries clear.

Christmas tree card

YOU WILL NEED

• Cream creative hammer card • Tacky tape™ film • Star punch 1.5cm (⅝in) • Bugle beads 7mm, 5g in gold and 2g in red • Seed beads size 9 (2.5mm), 5g each in lime, dark green and red • Medium and fine accent beads, 10g in green, red and gold • Craft knife and cutting mat • Embossing tool • Tweezers

1 Make a single-fold card from cream hammer-finish card, large enough to fit the motif, so there is about 1.5cm (⅝in) all round. For the Christmas tree, a card 11 x 17cm (4¼ x 6¾in) is ideal. Trace the tree template on page 107 on to tacky tape film and cut out, separating the tree from the pot. Open out the card, peel the backing paper off the tacky tape and stick the tree and pot motifs in the middle of the left-hand side.

Cut all the sections separately from the tacky tape film and then reassemble on the card. This lets you peel off one piece of protective top paper at a time to create the different coloured areas.

2 Punch a small star from tacky tape film and stick it at the top of the tree (peel back the tree paper slightly). Mark the centre vertical line on the left-hand side and use an embossing tool to score the card above and below the tree motif. Lay the card on a cutting mat and cut from the score line around the edge of the star, tree and pot.

3 Fold the card along the score line so that the tree pops out. Peel off the tree paper only and use tweezers to position gold bugles in draping lines across the tree about 2cm (¾in) apart. Punch five stars from tacky tape film, peel off the backing paper and stick them between the lines of bugles. Leave the protective top paper in position at this stage.

If there are details such as the stars within the larger motif, leave the star protective top paper in position until the background is filled in and then lift the paper off with the tip of a craft knife and decorate the stars.

4 Sprinkle lime and dark green seed beads all over the tree and tip off the excess. Sprinkle medium green accent beads over the tree and tip off the excess. Now pour fine green accent beads all over the tree, rub gently with your finger to fill all the gaps and then tip off any excess.

5 Peel off the top paper off the pot and arrange red bugle beads around the edge of the pot using tweezers. Sprinkle red seed beads over the pot and tip off excess. Peel off the star papers from the tree and sprinkle medium red accent beads over the stars and pot. Tip off the excess. Repeat with fine red accent beads and rub gently with your finger to fill all the gaps. Tip off excess.

6 Peel off the top star protective paper and decorate with medium and fine gold accent beads. Punch four stars from tacky tape film, peel off the backing and stick down the right-hand side of the card. Finish by decorating the stars with red seed beads and red accent beads.

Ring the changes

CHRISTMAS GREETINGS

To make these two cards you will need: suitable single-fold cards; tacky tape; the same bead selection as the Christmas tree card; multi-surface paint or strong glue. Use the templates on page 107.

Pudding card

Cut out the holly leaves from the top of the pudding with a craft knife and separate the icing, cake and plate sections before arranging them on the card. Position the 'raisins' on the pudding before filling in the background. Attach the holly berry seed beads with multi-surface paint or strong glue.

Snowman card

Punch out three 'buttons' from tacky tape and stick on the body. Arrange the scarf fringe and outline bugle beads before filling in the background. Create the facial features and the stripes on the scarf before applying the background beads.

Wrapped in style

THERE IS NOTHING MORE ENJOYABLE THAN GETTING A BEAUTIFULLY WRAPPED PRESENT AND WHEN THE WRAPPING INCLUDES A LOVELY BEAD CHARM IT'S REALLY SUCH A PLEASURE TO OPEN. THIS STUNNING EMBELLISHMENT MAY SEEM RATHER EXTRAVAGANT BUT IF YOU THINK OF IT AS A WAY TO USE UP ODD BEADS IN YOUR COLLECTION IT'S REALLY A SUPER IDEA AND IF YOU ATTACH A SWIVEL HOOK UNDER THE RIBBONS, THE BEADS CAN BE USED AS A HANDBAG CHARM ONCE THE GIFT IS UNWRAPPED – TWO GIFTS FOR THE PRICE OF ONE!

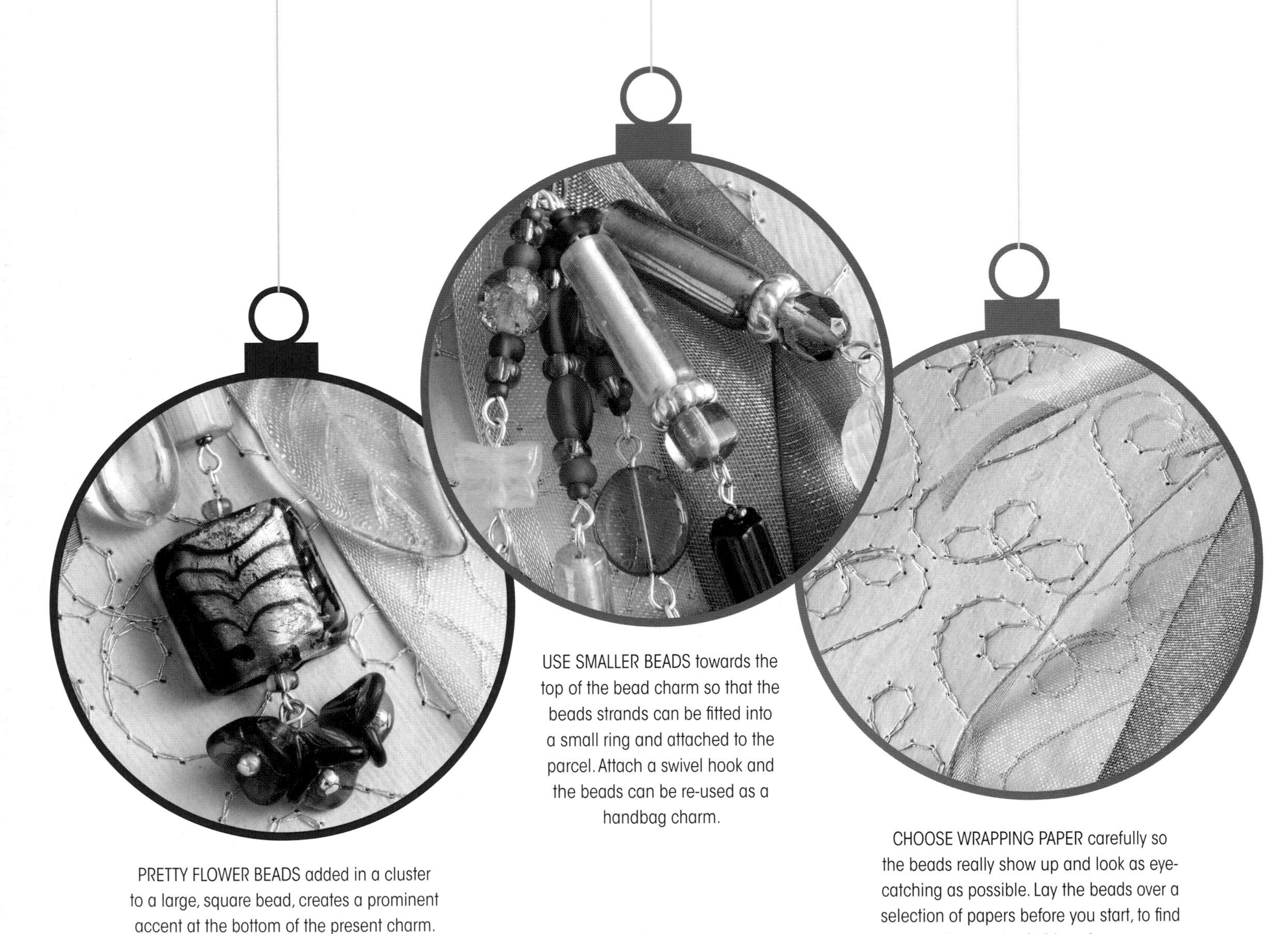

USE SMALLER BEADS towards the top of the bead charm so that the beads strands can be fitted into a small ring and attached to the parcel. Attach a swivel hook and the beads can be re-used as a handbag charm.

PRETTY FLOWER BEADS added in a cluster to a large, square bead, creates a prominent accent at the bottom of the present charm.

CHOOSE WRAPPING PAPER carefully so the beads really show up and look as eye-catching as possible. Lay the beads over a selection of papers before you start, to find the most suitable colour.

Present charm

YOU WILL NEED

• Large decorative beads 1–2cm, five • Tubular beads 5 x 20mm, four • Round crystals 5 x 20mm, five • Smaller decorative beads 5mm–1cm, five • Mixed seed beads 2–4mm, twelve • Pendant or droplet beads 15–20mm long, five • Leaf bead 20 x 35mm • Flower bead charms 7 x 10mm, three • Silver beads 2mm, eight • Silver ring spacers 8mm, five • Silver-plated wire, 0.6mm (24swg) • Triangle or pendant bails 9mm • Silver split ring 7mm (⅜in) • Swivel hook (optional)

1 Collect together a selection of beads in toning colours – I used a mix of purple, silver-lined, pink and crystal. You will need some beads to fit on the end of each strand, such as pendant beads, droplets or teardrops. Beads that have a hole at one end are fixed using a triangle or pendant bail. Simply open the bail slightly, slot in the bead and squeeze the ends together so that the prongs go into the hole of the bead.

2 When droplets or other decorative beads have a hole that goes down through the centre of the bead use a headpin to make the attachment. Feed the bead on to the headpin so that the wider end is at the bottom. Hold the headpin in round-nosed pliers and bend the wire round to make a ring (see Techniques page 102). Snip off the tail and straighten the ring.

If the hole in the bead is too big for the headpin, pick up a seed bead first and then add the drop bead.

3 The other beads on the present charm are added using a wire link. To make a link cut about 20cm (8in) of 0.6mm silver-plated wire. Make a ring at one end of the wire using round-nosed pliers (see Techniques page 101).

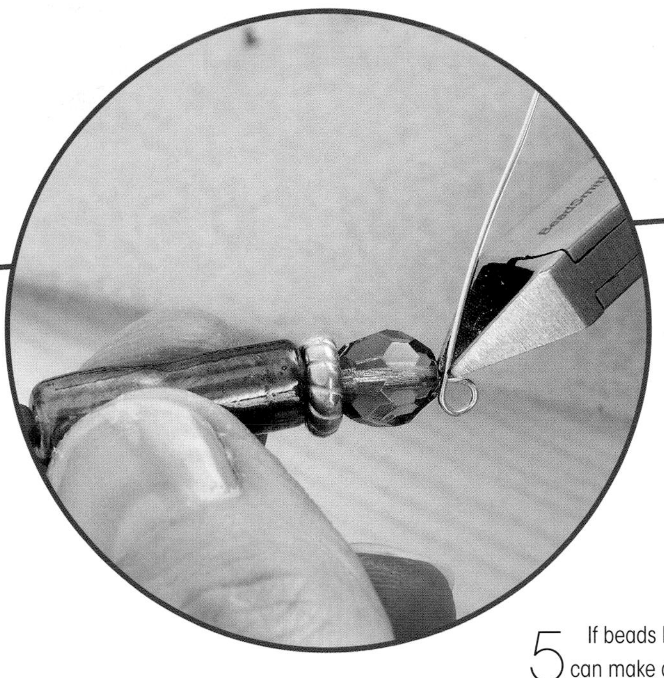

4 Pick up several seed beads on to the prepared wire, let them drop down and make a ring at the other end. Snip off the excess wire and straighten the loop. Make the top links slightly thinner, adding seed beads at one end instead so that they hang close together.

When adding a silver ring bead, pick up a small silver ball bead that fits inside the ring before picking up the next decorative bead. The silver ball is hidden inside the ring but holds it centrally on the wire link.

5 If beads have a large hole you can make a slightly different link to support the bead. Make a loop of wire with round-nosed pliers and then wind the tail around the wire several times to make a tight spiral. Trim off the tail. Thread on the bead and repeat the process at the other end. Make a selection of beads on wire links, some from large beads and others with long tubular beads. Use silver rings to add a touch of silver to some of the links.

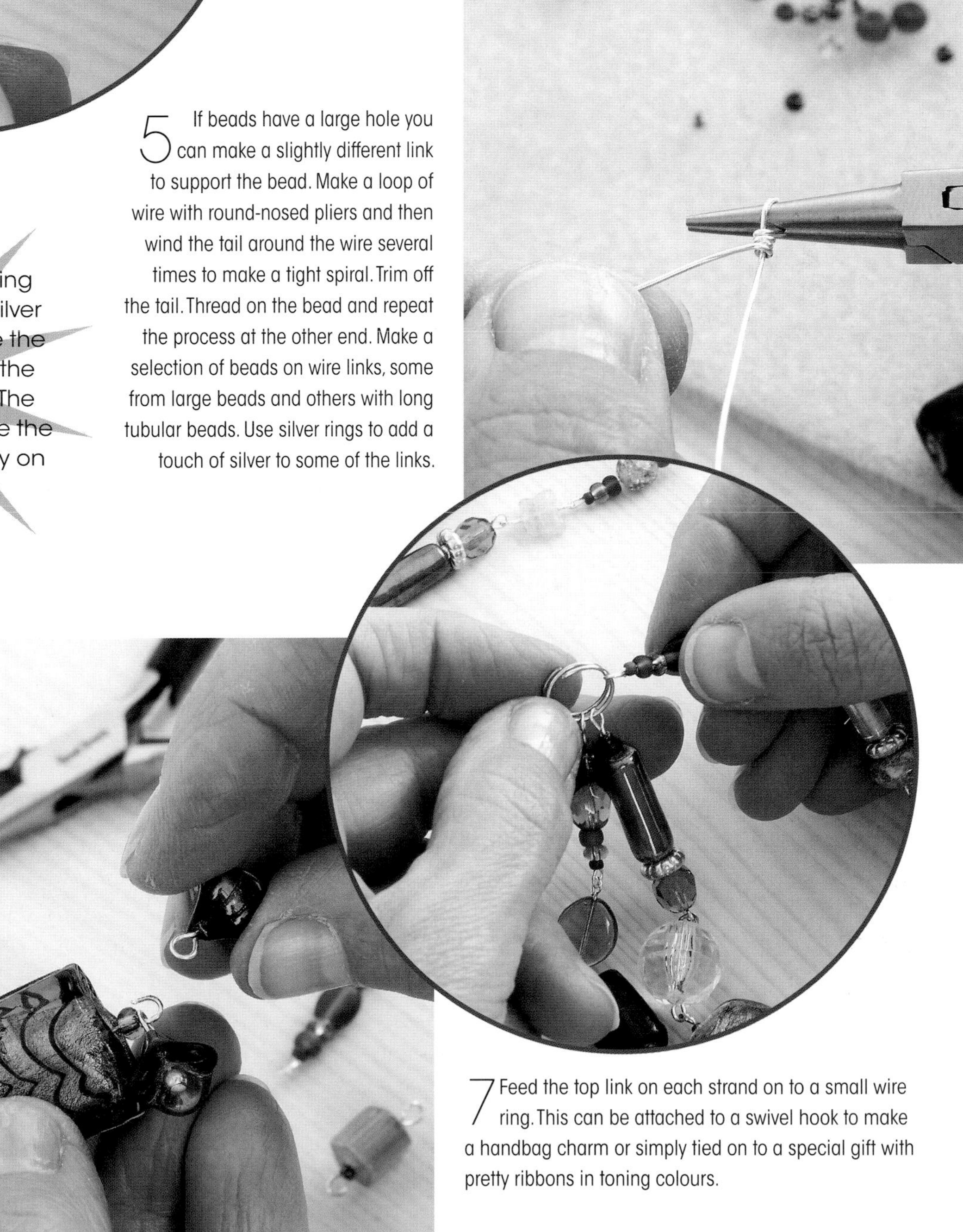

6 Begin to join all the links together beginning with thinner links at the top and adding larger accent beads further down. Make five strands in all ranging from about 10–15cm (4–6in). Vary the position of the larger beads to get an attractive balance on all five strands. For a prominent accent at the end of the longest strand attach several flower bead charms, made with headpins, on to the same wire link.

7 Feed the top link on each strand on to a small wire ring. This can be attached to a swivel hook to make a handbag charm or simply tied on to a special gift with pretty ribbons in toning colours.

Going crackers

SETTING THE TABLE FOR THE CHRISTMAS MEAL IS ALWAYS A DELIGHTFUL TASK AS IT ALL LOOKS SO GORGEOUS WITH PRETTY NAPKINS AND CANDLES, AND THESE FANTASTIC CRACKERS ARE SURE TO GET THE CELEBRATION GOING WITH A BANG! GUESTS WILL BE ABLE TO TAKE THE BEADED MOTIF HOME AS A MEMENTO AND CAN MAKE IT INTO A BROOCH OR PENDANT. CRÊPE PAPER IS THE IDEAL PAPER FOR CRACKERS AS IT HOLDS ITS SHAPE SO WELL – CHOOSE GORGEOUS SILVER FOR A TRULY OPULENT LOOK OR MAKE FUN CRACKERS FOR CHILDREN IN GOLD AND BRIGHT RED WITH A DELIGHTFUL BEADED FAIRY OR ROBIN (SEE PAGE 93).

SEED BEADS in a contrast colour draw the eye to the star shape in the middle of the heart motif and add an extra Christmassy feel. Add a matching crystal droplet to the point as a finishing touch.

THE TINY STAR MOTIF, which is created by the juxtaposition of the five centre crystals, can be seen clearly if you choose a deep-coloured silk dupion to wrap around the cracker.

EXQUISITE FABRICS such as a richly coloured silk dupion give a luxury finish to the crackers. Ruche the fabric to create interesting textures and finish with wrapped beaded wires.

Star cracker

YOU WILL NEED

(for cracker) • Cardboard tube from kitchen roll or similar • Silver crêpe paper • Lilac glitter lace-effect paper • Double-sided adhesive tape • Thin card • Scraps of burgundy silk dupion

(for beaded star motif) • Swarovski bicone AB crystals 6mm, five • Swarovski flower AB crystals 6mm, five • Swarovski bicone AB crystals 15 x 6mm, five • Swarovski bicone AB crystals 5mm, twenty-five • Seed beads size 9 (2.5mm), silver-lined crystal, 5g • Silver-plated wire, 1m (1yd) of 0.315mm (30swg)

1 To make the cracker, cut one piece of tubing 11cm (4¼in) and another two pieces 5cm (2in) long. Cut a piece of silver crêpe paper 20 x 42cm (8 x 16½in) with the creases going lengthways. Lay the long tube in the middle of the crêpe and the shorter pieces at each end. Stick an 11cm (4¼in) length of double-sided tape centrally along one edge of the crêpe and a short piece opposite the shorter tubes. Peel off the tape backing paper and roll the crêpe up to fit snugly around the three tubes.

A bread knife is the ideal tool to cut card tubes – place the tube on a breadboard and use a sawing action.

2 Make sure the centre tube is in the middle and then squeeze the crêpe paper between the tubes to create the cracker shape. Tie a short length of wire or thread between the tubes to secure. If you want to add a hat, tiny gift and cracker-bang strip into the cracker, tuck them inside now before you secure the ends.

3 Pull the crêpe paper between your fingers to stretch the edge and create a softly fluted effect. Wrap a 9.5 x 20cm (3¾ x 8in) piece of lilac lacy paper around the centre tube and stick on the reverse side.

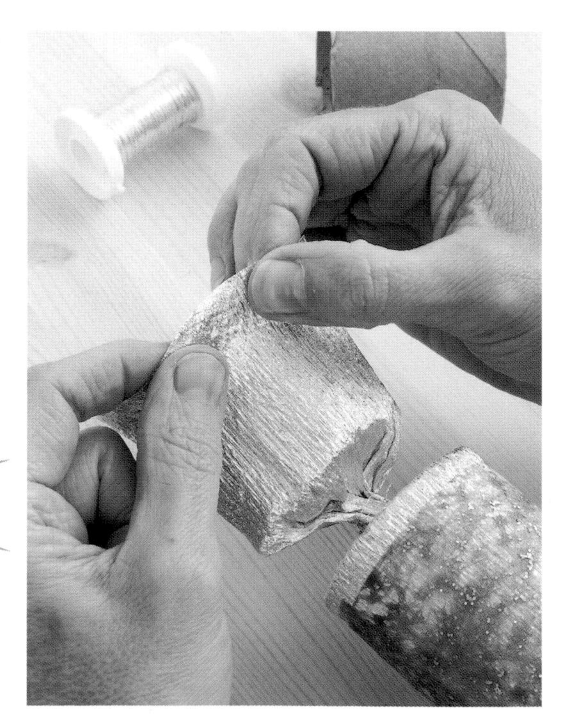

For a quick and easy finish, wrap a length of wide ribbon around the cracker instead of silk and then tie narrower ribbons at each end.

4 Cut a 5.5 x 18cm (2¼ x 7in) piece of thin card and cover one side with double-sided tape. Stick a larger piece of silk dupion over the tape so that it is ruched and then stick the raw side edges on the reverse side. Put the cracker aside while you make the beaded star motif.

5 To make the beaded star motif, pick up 5 of the 6mm bicone crystals on a 50cm (20in) length of silver-plated wire and let them drop down to the middle. Take one end of the wire through the last crystal and pull taut to make a circle. * On one end of the wire pick up 4 seed beads, a flower crystal and a seed bead. Take the wire back through the flower crystal and pick up 4 more seed beads. Take the wire back through the bicone crystal to create the first point of the star.

6 Take the wire through the next crystal and repeat from * (in step 5) to make the next star point. Repeat all the way round to create a five-pointed star.

7 Take the longer tail of the wire and pick up a 15 x 6mm crystal and a seed bead. Missing the seed bead, feed the wire back down the long crystal and through the next bicone crystal. Add a long crystal between each of the points of the star. Twist the wires together, trim and tuck away on the reverse side.

8 Cut 20cm (8in) of wire and feed it through the seed beads on one of the points of the star, leaving a short tail. Pick up a 5mm bicone, a seed bead and a bicone crystal and feed the wire through the seed bead at the top of the next long crystal.

9 To add the extra crystal and seed bead at each point of the star, when you get to the second point pick up a 5mm bicone and a seed bead. Take the end of the wire back through the bicone crystal just added and through the seed bead at the top of the long crystal again. Work around the motif adding 2 crystals and a seed bead between the long crystals and the points of the centre star, and an extra bicone crystal and seed bead at each of the outer points. Feed the ends of the wires through several beads so that they overlap and then twist around between beads and trim neatly.

Sew the bead motif to the middle of the cracker band and then wrap the band around the cracker and sew or stick along the back seam. Wrap strips of silk to cover the wire ties and then decorate with beaded wire to finish (see the red tag on page 67).

Heart cracker

YOU WILL NEED

(for cracker - see list on page 88)

(for beaded heart motif) • Swarovski bicone AB crystals 6mm, five • Swarovski flower AB crystals 6mm, five • Swarovski bicone AB crystals 15 x 6mm, three • Swarovski bicone AB crystals 5mm, twenty • Swarovski droplet, lilac crystal 12 x 6mm • Seed beads size 10 (2.2mm), colour-lined lilac, 5g • Silver-plated wire 1m (1yd) of 0.315mm (30swg)

1 Make the cracker by following steps 1–4 (page 88) of the star cracker and continue to create the centre beaded star by following steps 5–7 but using lilac colour-lined seed beads and AB crystals. To support the shape of the heart motif add 3 long crystals only, as follows: on the longer tail of the wire pick up a 15 x 6mm crystal and a seed bead. Feed the wire back down the long crystal and then through 2 bicone crystals. Add another long crystal and then take the wire through the next bicone crystal and add a third long crystal.

2 Cut a new 40cm (16in) length of wire and feed it through the seed bead at the top of the star (directly opposite the single long crystal). Pick up 4 bicone crystals with a lilac seed bead between each one. Take the wire through the seed bead on the end of the long crystal. Pick up another 4 bicone crystals and 3 seed beads and take the wire through one of the bottom points of the star. Finally, pick up 2 bicone crystals with a seed bead in the middle.

3 Take the wire through the seed bead at the end of the bottom long crystal. Pick up 2 lilac seed beads, a lilac crystal droplet and 2 lilac seed beads and take the wire back through the seed bead on the end of the long crystal. Work the second side of the heart in the same way, secure the wire ends and trim neatly.

Attach the beaded motif to the cracker as described in the final paragraph in step 9 on page 89.

Fairy cracker

YOU WILL NEED

(for cracker) • Gold and cream crêpe paper • A4 pinky-red polypropylene sheet or heavy vellum • Red rickrack braid and sparkly cord

(for beaded fairy) • Seed beads size 11 (2mm), 5g each of copper, cream and brown and fourteen red • Bugles 8mm, twelve cream • Silver-plated wire, 0.25mm (34swg)

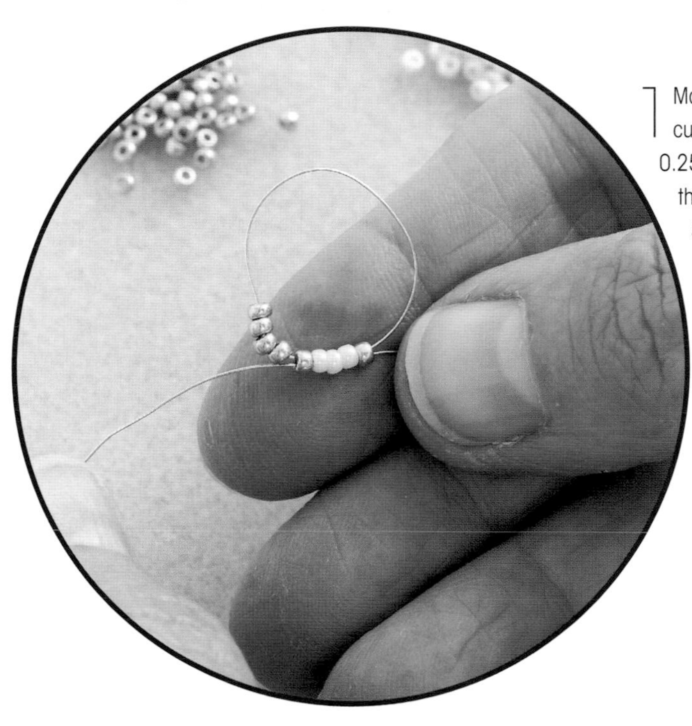

1 Make the beaded fairy by first cutting a 75cm (30in) length of 0.25mm (34swg) wire. Referring to the bead diagram below, pick up 5 copper beads, 3 cream beads and another copper bead and let them drop down to the middle of the wire. Take one end of the wire back through a copper bead, 3 cream beads and a copper bead again. Pull up taut and flatten the circle to create two rows of beads.

These fun fairy and robin crackers (see picture on page 93) are made in the same way as the adult version but with gold crêpe paper, rickrack braid and sparkly cord to finish.

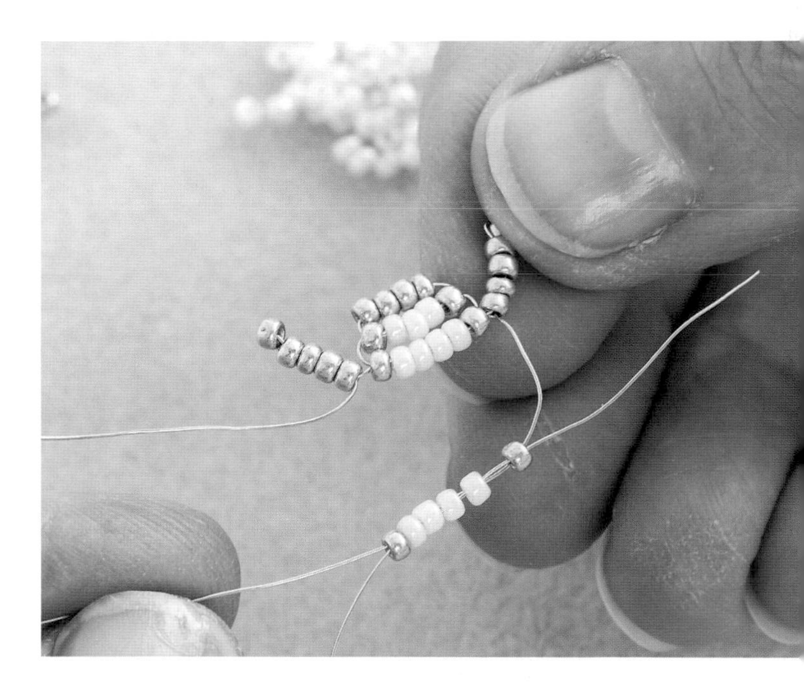

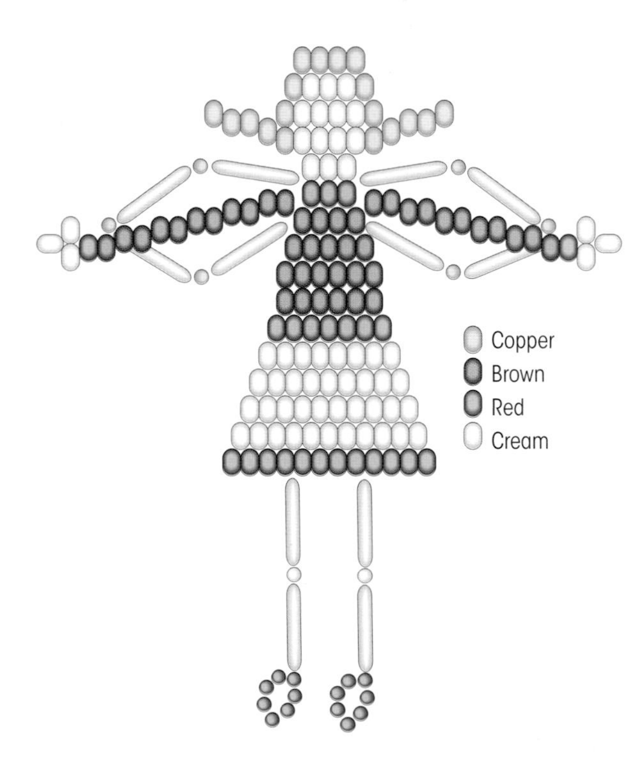

Fairy beading diagram

2 Pick up a copper bead, 4 cream and a copper bead on one end of the wire and feed the other wire through the beads from the opposite direction. To make the pigtails, pick up 5 copper beads on one end, miss the last bead and feed the wire back down the other four beads. Repeat on the other side to make the second pigtail. Continue following the bead diagram to complete the body, adding arms in the same way as the pigtails. Wind the ends of the wire around the side wire to secure and trim neatly.

3 Cut a new 20cm (8in) length of wire and feed it through the centre four beads on the bottom of the dress. Pick up a long cream bugle, a cream seed bead, another long bugle and 7 red seed beads. Take the wire back up through the 'leg' and wind the wire around between the beads to secure at the top. Make a second leg in the same way and trim excess wire.

4 Attach a new 20cm (8in) length of wire by feeding it through a row of beads in the middle of the fairy's top. Pick up a four cream bugles with cream seed beads in between. Bend the wire to a wing shape and then secure the wire around the edge of the fairy's body as before. Trim the ends neatly.

Children can make the little beaded figures themselves and once they learn the simple technique can have fun designing all sorts of different creatures

5 Make the cracker with the gold crêpe paper following steps 1–4 on page 88. Cut a 10 x 20cm (4 x 8in) strip of cream crêpe paper with the crinkle texture going widthways. Stretch the long edges and then stick around the cracker. Cut 7 x 20cm (2¾ x 8in) strips of pinky-red polypropylene and stick around the middle. Decorate with rickrack braid and tie sparkly cord around to finish. Attach the beaded motif with glue dots.

Ring the changes

ROBIN CRACKER

To make the beaded robin motif you will need: a black seed bead for the eye; 5g of brown seed beads; small quantities of red and copper seed beads; four 8mm brown bugles and eight 6mm brown bugles; 1.5m (1½yd) of 0.25mm (34swg) silver-plated wire.

Referring to the bead diagram here, begin the robin motif by picking up 17 brown, 5 red and 15 brown seed beads on a 1m (40in) length of wire. Drop the beads down to the middle of the wire and take an end through the fifteen beads just added and three red beads. Pull the beads taut and then follow the bead diagram to make the rest of the body. Feed new pieces of wire through some of the beads on the top row to add the head and tail and then make the beak and add it separately too. Add new wire for the legs as indicated on the diagram. Make a cracker and attach the bead motif as described for the fairy (step 5 above).

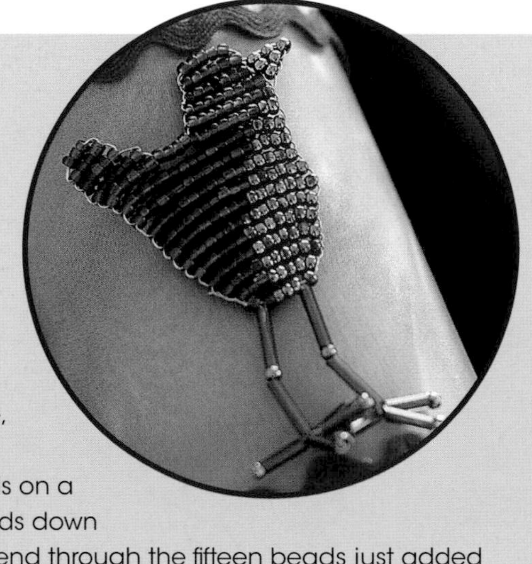

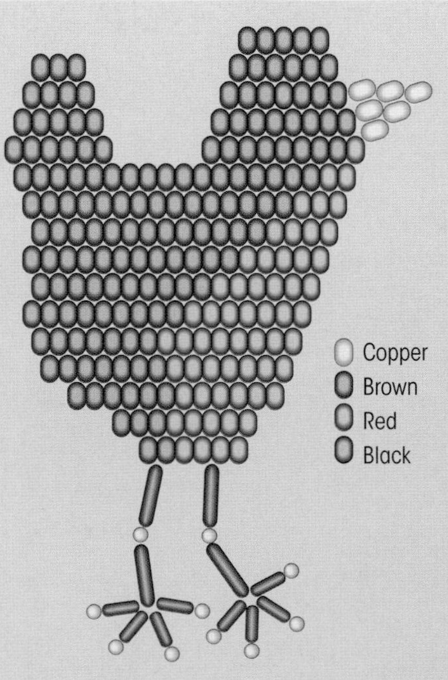

Robin beading diagram

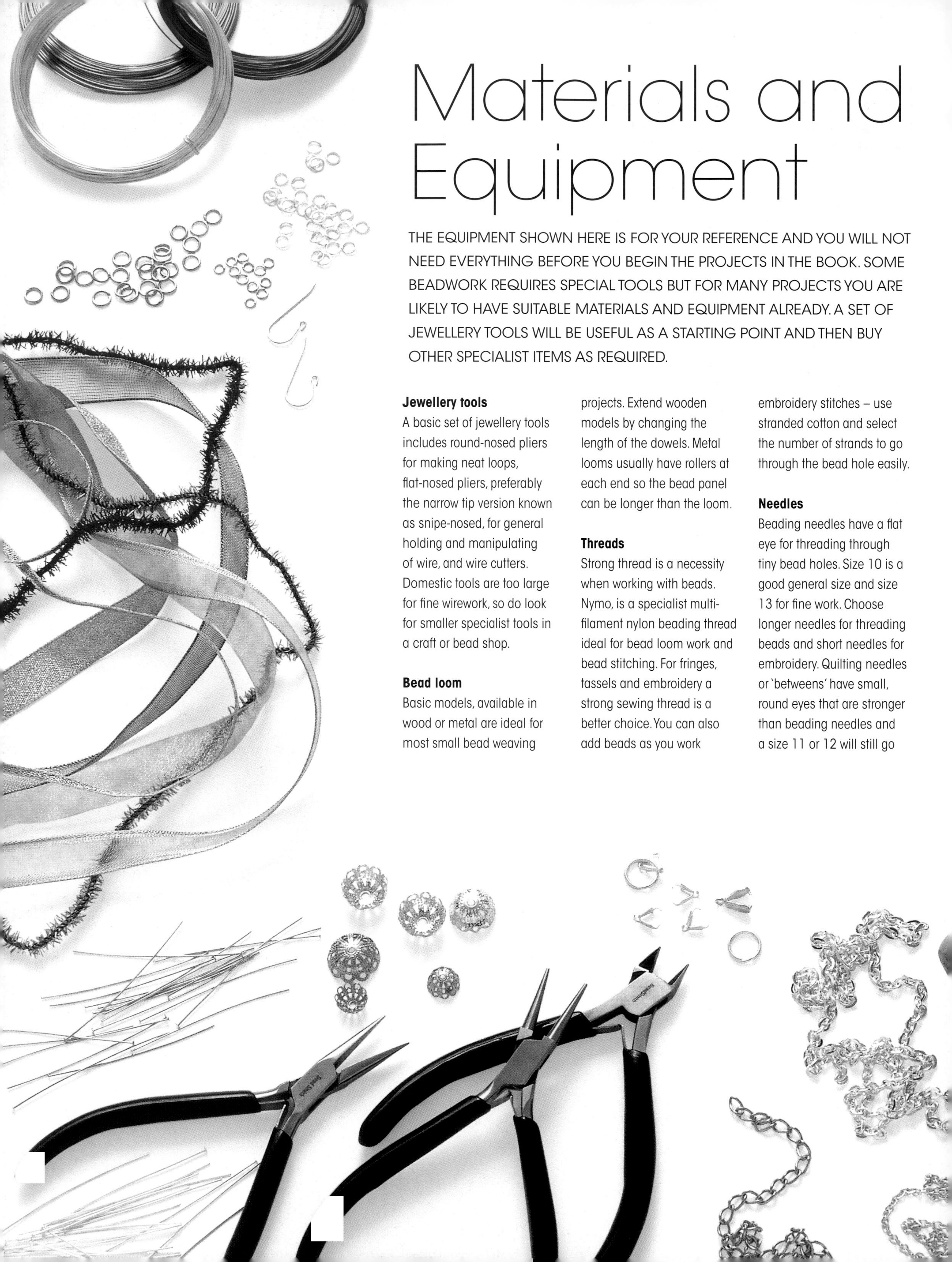

Materials and Equipment

THE EQUIPMENT SHOWN HERE IS FOR YOUR REFERENCE AND YOU WILL NOT NEED EVERYTHING BEFORE YOU BEGIN THE PROJECTS IN THE BOOK. SOME BEADWORK REQUIRES SPECIAL TOOLS BUT FOR MANY PROJECTS YOU ARE LIKELY TO HAVE SUITABLE MATERIALS AND EQUIPMENT ALREADY. A SET OF JEWELLERY TOOLS WILL BE USEFUL AS A STARTING POINT AND THEN BUY OTHER SPECIALIST ITEMS AS REQUIRED.

Jewellery tools

A basic set of jewellery tools includes round-nosed pliers for making neat loops, flat-nosed pliers, preferably the narrow tip version known as snipe-nosed, for general holding and manipulating of wire, and wire cutters. Domestic tools are too large for fine wirework, so do look for smaller specialist tools in a craft or bead shop.

Bead loom

Basic models, available in wood or metal are ideal for most small bead weaving projects. Extend wooden models by changing the length of the dowels. Metal looms usually have rollers at each end so the bead panel can be longer than the loom.

Threads

Strong thread is a necessity when working with beads. Nymo, is a specialist multi-filament nylon beading thread ideal for bead loom work and bead stitching. For fringes, tassels and embroidery a strong sewing thread is a better choice. You can also add beads as you work embroidery stitches – use stranded cotton and select the number of strands to go through the bead hole easily.

Needles

Beading needles have a flat eye for threading through tiny bead holes. Size 10 is a good general size and size 13 for fine work. Choose longer needles for threading beads and short needles for embroidery. Quilting needles or 'betweens' have small, round eyes that are stronger than beading needles and a size 11 or 12 will still go through most seed beads. Sharps have longer eyes that bulge slightly and are not suitable for beadwork.

Jewellery findings
These are the metal bits that make beadwork into jewellery. You can buy most items in silver- or gold-plated or in more expensive pure metal. You may need earring findings, fastenings, clasps, jump rings, bails and headpins. Everything you need is listed with each project and is available from bead and craft shops.

Wire and chain
Craft and jewellery wire is generally copper based, with plating for silver and gold, or enamelling for a wide range of colours. This wire is soft and easy to bend. Thickness is in millimetres or standard wire gauge (swg). One of the finest is 0.2mm or 36swg, while 0.8mm or 21swg is thicker; so the smaller the swg, the thicker the wire. Chain is readily available in a wide range of styles, colours and weights.

Ribbons and cord
Satin, velvet, organza and grosgrain are just a few of the gorgeous ribbon types that can be used with bead projects to make them look absolutely stunning. Choose wire-edged ribbon if you need it to hold its shape. Look out for interesting cords and ribbons specially made for Christmas on cardmaking and scrapbook websites.

Glues and adhesives
Sticking beads and wire can be a little tricky because of their smooth surfaces. A low-melt glue gun is useful when you can hide the glue behind the design, otherwise use specialist jewellery adhesive that dries clear or fast-acting glue such as gel superglue.

Techniques

MOST OF THE PROJECTS HAVE FULL STEP-BY-STEP INSTRUCTIONS THAT ALLOW YOU TO COMPLETE THE ITEM FROM THE PROJECT PAGES BUT THIS SECTION IS USEFUL IF YOU ARE NEW TO BEADWORK. IT PROVIDES GREATER DETAIL FOR BEAD LOOM WORK, EMBROIDERY AND WIREWORK, WHICH WILL GIVE YOU GREATER UNDERSTANDING AND TIPS FOR BETTER RESULTS. THERE ARE ALSO DIAGRAMS FOR SOME OF THE COMMONLY USED STITCHES AND KNOTS.

USING A BEAD LOOM

A bead loom is used to create flat bands of beading. The width of the band is determined by the width of the loom, and as you space the threads to fit the beads in between, the size of the beads will affect the loom size. Bead looms are usually threaded with a strong thread such as Nymo, but you can use metallic threads for a sparkly effect and even fine wire so that the band of beads can be shaped like the bead twist decorations on page 44.

1 Count the beads across the design and add one to find the number of warp threads required. Add 60cm (24in) to the finished length of the project for attaching the threads to the loom and finishing off. Cut the warp threads and tie an overhand knot (see page 100). Split the group of threads and loop over the pin on one roller.

2 Secure the roller and, holding the threads taut, arrange the threads along the spring. Use a large needle or 'T' pin to separate the threads. Leave gaps between the threads equal to the size of the beads. Line the threads up across the other spring in the same way so that they run parallel to one another and don't cross at any point.

3 Holding the threads taut, (a piece of adhesive tape will stop the threads coming off the spring) tie an overhand knot near the end and loop the thread over the pin. Turn the roller to take up the excess thread. Adjust the thread between the rollers so that there is sufficient on the top roller to finish off.

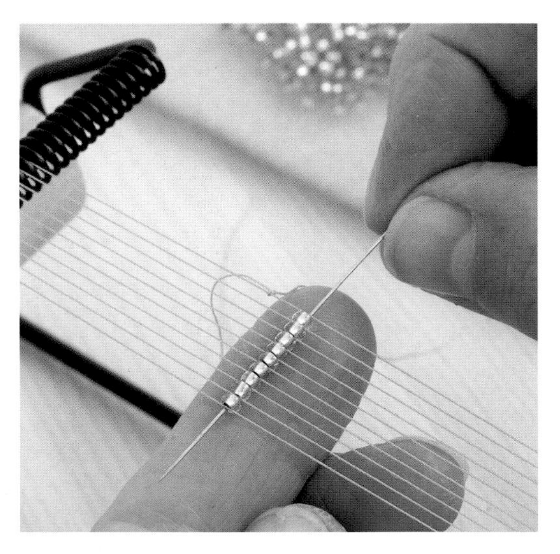

4 Thread a long beading needle with a 2m (2yd) length of thread and tie to the outer warp thread on one side. Pick up the required number of beads in the right order. Hold the beads under the warp threads and push them up between the threads so that there is a thread either side of each bead.

5 Pull the needle through the beads, keeping them in position with your finger, as shown, and then feed the needle back through the beads from the opposite side. This time the needle goes above the warp threads. Pull the thread taut and pick up the next row of beads and repeat the process.

6 Continue adding rows of beads in the same way making sure that the weft thread, which is on the needle, passes above each warp thread as it passes back through the beads. After the first few rows it will become much easier to work. Follow the project chart, picking up the beads in the right order to create the design.

7 When about 13cm (5in) of thread is left on the weft thread, remove the needle and leave the thread hanging. Thread a new length and feed through the same beads leaving a similar tail. Continue the beadwork and sew in both ends later, securing the threads with a half hitch knot (see page 100) before trimming the ends.

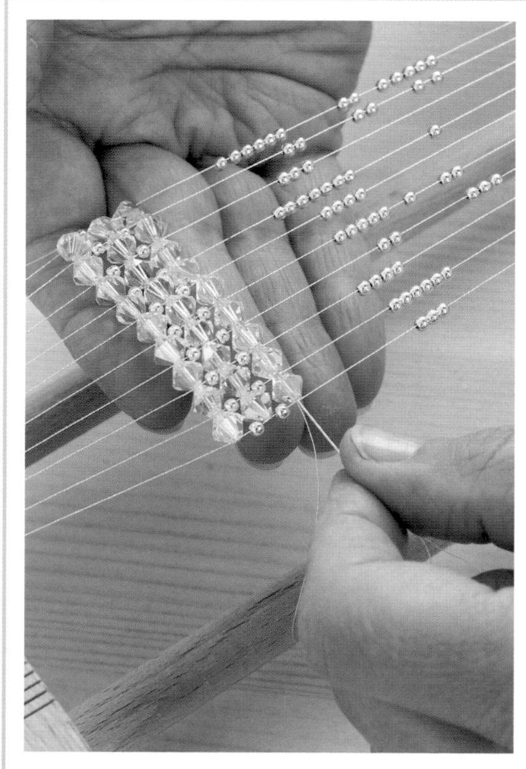

Christmas stocking

For this stocking on page 54, beads were pre-threaded on to the warp threads before setting up the loom. The small beads fill the gap between the bicone crystals and create a more ornate border. To find out if beads will fit together in this way arrange a few rows on a beading mat before setting up on the loom.

BEAD EMBROIDERY

You can add beads of all shapes and sizes with bead embroidery. Beads can be added singly or in lines and be incorporated with hand embroidery stitches for a really ornate effect.
On fine fabrics use a backing fabric to support the weight of the beads and to give somewhere to anchor the threads. Always secure threads carefully so that the beads don't fall off.

Preparing the fabric

1 If you layer a piece of thin wadding (batting) between the top fabric and a thin backing fabric you do not need to use an embroidery frame or hoop. The backing fabric is needed so that you can anchor threads on the reverse side. It should launder in the same way as the top fabric and be pre-shrunk to prevent the finished item puckering when washed.

2 Cut out the shape of the panel with added seam allowances in all three layers. Pin the layers together and tack (baste) around the outside to hold in position. If the item you are embroidering is quite large, tack across the panel in straight or diagonal lines.

3 To begin or finish the thread for beading, work two small backstitches on the reverse side. When working on felt it isn't necessary to have either a backing fabric or wadding. The felt fabric is firm enough to prevent puckering and thick enough to prevent the backstitches showing on the right side.

Adding single beads

Choose a thread colour to match the bead or the background fabric and work with a double length for strength. To prevent the beads pulling out if they are widely spaced, work a second stitch through each bead before attaching the next.

Draw any motifs using an embroidery marker. Secure a double thread on the reverse side and bring the needle through to the right side. Pick up a bead and take the needle back through a bead's width away.

COUCHING

From the French verb 'se coucher', to lie down, couching is used to apply a string of beads in a straight or curved line. You can use two separate threads – one for stringing the beads and one for couching but this quick method is ideal for small motifs.

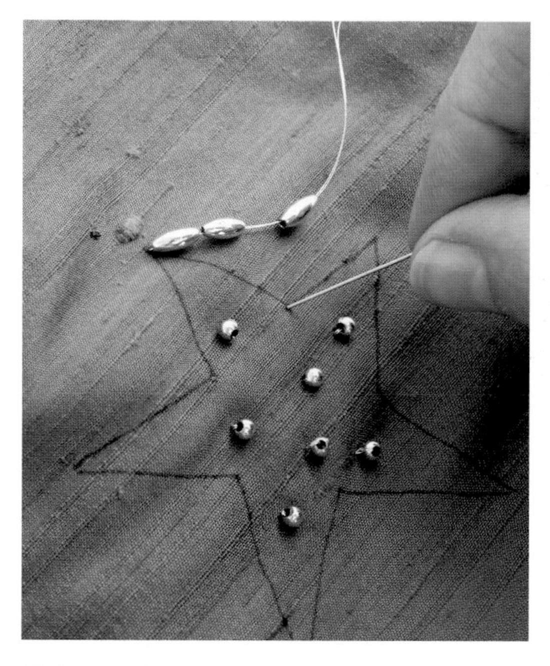

1 Secure a double thread on the reverse side and bring the beading needle out at the end of one line. Pick up the required number of beads to fill the line with a little ease and take the needle back through at the other end.

2 Bring the needle back out between the first two beads on one side of the laid thread and take it back through on the other side so that the beads are caught down on to the fabric. Work a couching stitch between each bead if they are long like these oat beads or between every two or three seed beads.

BACKSTITCH

Backstitch is ideal for adding a few beads in a row or for working long lines of beads. Pick up only two or three beads at a time to work a curved line but on a straight line add four or five beads, taking the needle back through the last two each time.

1 Bring the beading needle out on the right side where the bead line is to begin. Pick up several beads on the thread and work a backstitch from the end of the bead line and go back two beads.

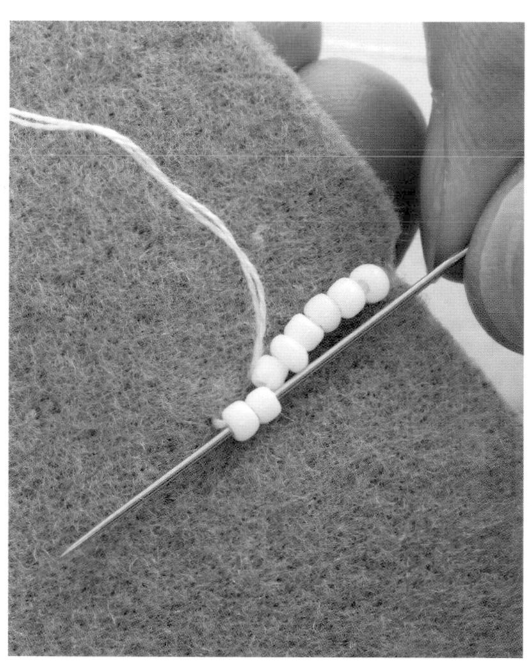

2 Take the needle back through the last two beads. Pick up the next group of beads and repeat the backstitch. Continue until the line is the length required.

EMBROIDERY STITCHES

You can add beads while you work a wide variety of embroidery stitches. Simple stitches like buttonhole stitch, herringbone stitch, coral stitch and fly stitch work well but you can experiment with all sorts of stitches.

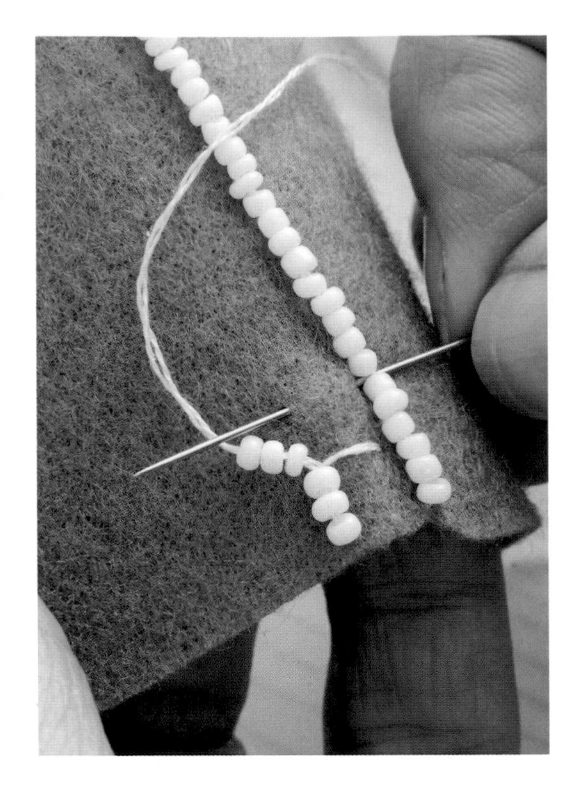

Bring the beading needle out ready to work the first embroidery stitch. Pick up the required number of beads to fit the stitch length. Work the embroidery stitch, manoeuvring the beads into position before you pull the thread taut.

KNOTS USED IN BEADING

There are several simple knots used in beading to anchor threads or to tie off ends securely. For extra security use a cocktail stick to drop a tiny amount of fixative on the knot, such as clear nail polish or a fray check liquid.

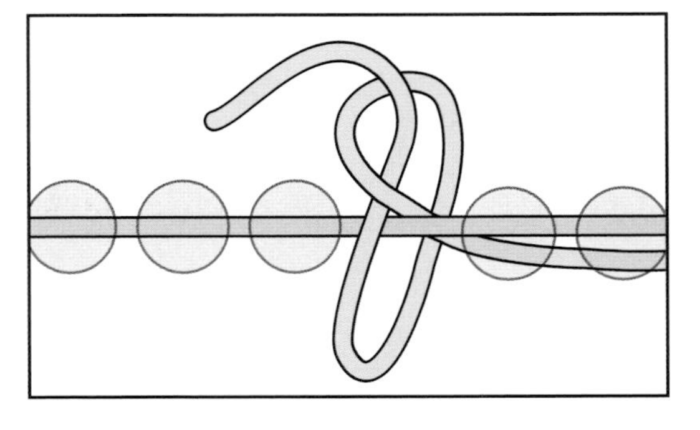

HALF HITCH KNOT

Use this knot to secure a thread in loom work or bead stitches. Work the knot between two beads and feed the end through several beads before trimming.

REEF (SQUARE) KNOT

This is the basic knot for joining two threads of equal thickness. Feed each end back through several beads before trimming the ends.

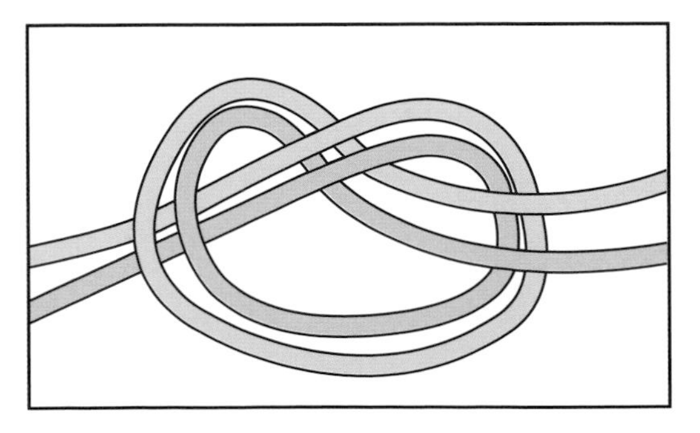

OVERHAND KNOT

Use this knot to tie threads together before fitting on a bead loom or to join two threads together at the edge of a piece of work. The knot can be moved into position with a needle.

WIREWORK

Many of the projects in the book use wire and jewellery techniques to add beads and sometimes it is difficult to see the details in the step-by-step photography. In this section the shots are really close up so that you can see exactly what is happening. For most of the wirework projects you will need a set of jewellery tools (see page 94 for advice on what to buy).

Making a loop

There are several ways to make a loop at the end of a piece of wire. Try all three methods shown here and overleaf to decide which you prefer or use them all. The first is often used to make an eyepin with soft craft wire to start a bead link; the second to make the loop at the other end of the bead link and the third for the harder wire found on headpins.

If you want a smaller loop hold the wire closer to the tip, and further down the jaws if you want a larger loop.

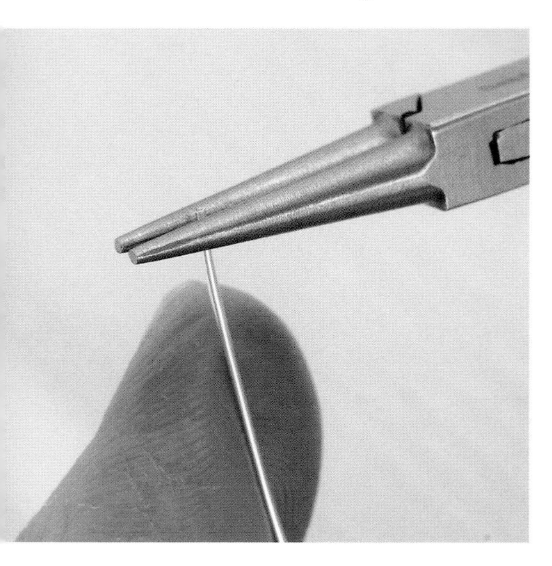

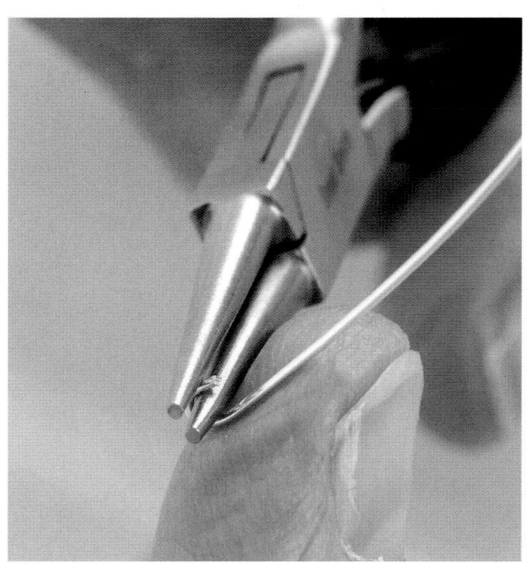

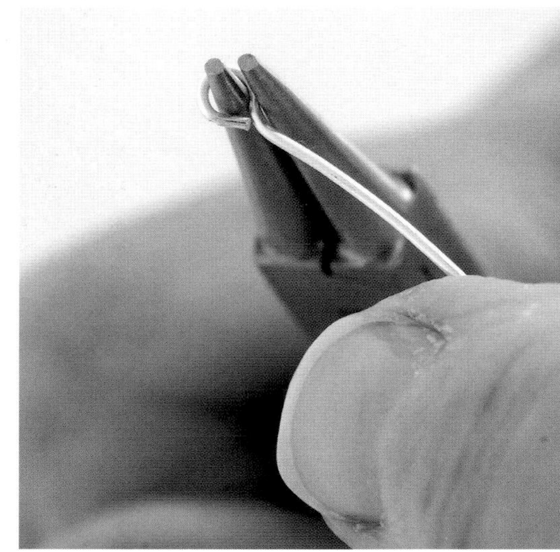

CRAFT WIRE LOOP

1 Hold the wire in the round-nosed pliers about 6mm (¼in) from the tip so that you can just feel the end of the wire if you run a finger along the jaws of the pliers.

2 Rotate the pliers so that the tail of the wire is sticking up in the air. Rotate the pliers back round and use your thumb to bend the wire around the jaws of the pliers until the wire touches the cut end on the other side.

3 Insert the round-nosed pliers in the loop so that the tail is between the jaws and bend the tail of the wire back slightly. The loop should be in the middle directly above the tail.

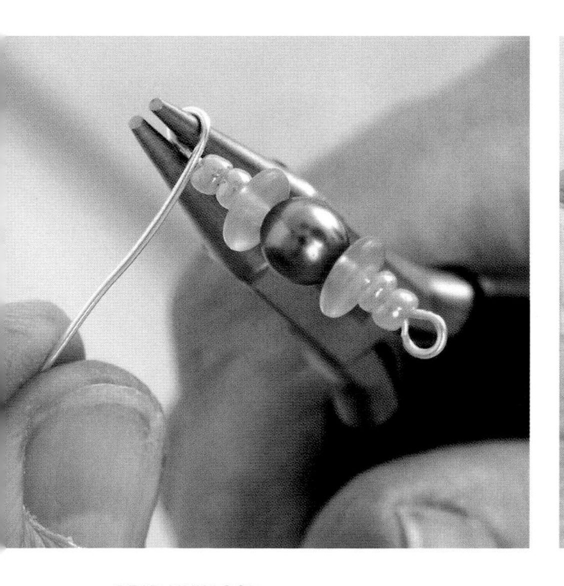

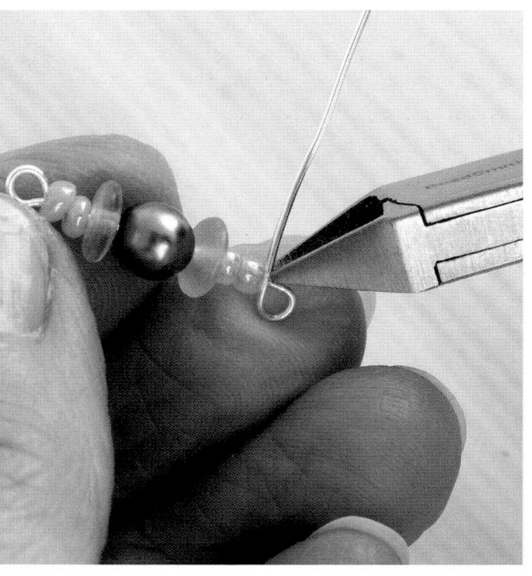

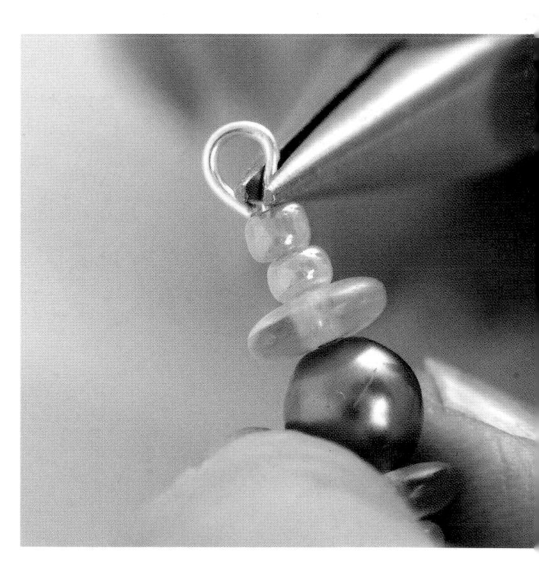

BEAD LINK LOOP

1 Pick up the beads that you want on the link. Hold the wire at the end of the beads so that there is a wire width between the beads and the pliers. Wind the wire around the jaws until it is straight down the other side.

2 Snip off the tail of the wire where it crosses over. Hold the flat side of the pliers next to the loop and use the very tip of the wire cutters to cut the tail off.

3 Use snipe-nosed or round-nosed pliers to bend the loop back a little so that it is straight. If necessary hold the loops at both ends and twist so they are level.

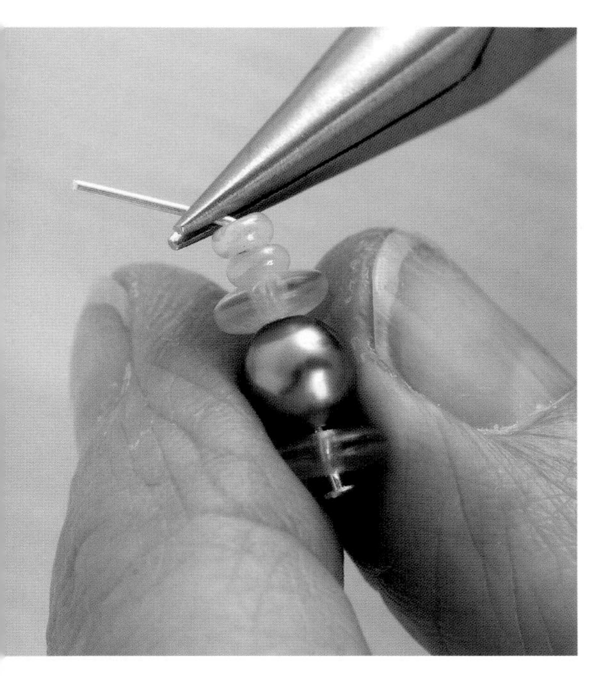

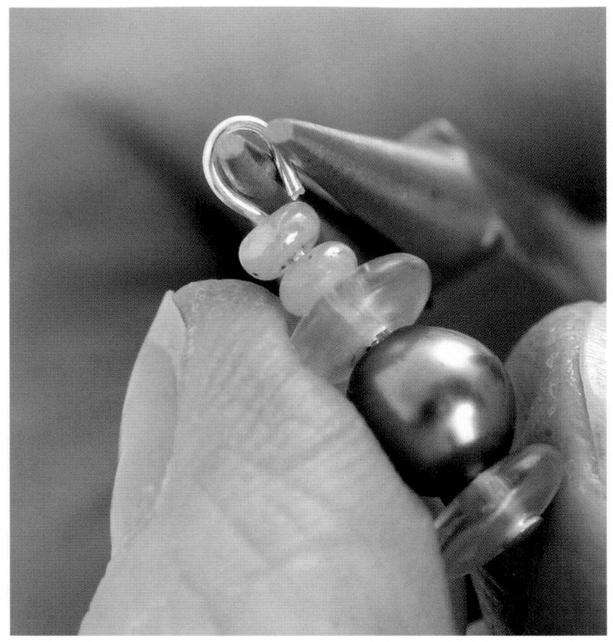

HEADPIN LOOP

1 Pick up the beads you require on the headpin. Trim the end of the headpin so that there is about 7–8mm (5⁄16in) above the beads. Bend the trimmed headpin at an angle close to the top of the beads.

2 Grasp the end of the headpin in the round-nosed pliers about 6mm (¼in) from the tips of the jaws. Rotate the pliers to make a round loop and bend the wire close to the hole in the top bead.

Opening and closing loops and jump rings

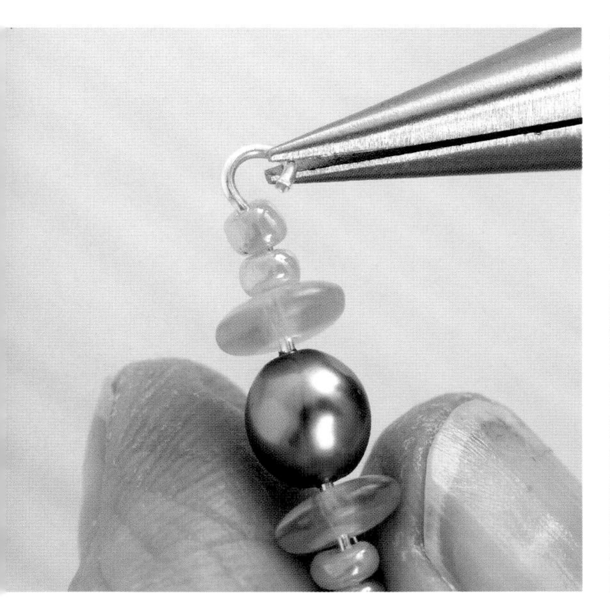

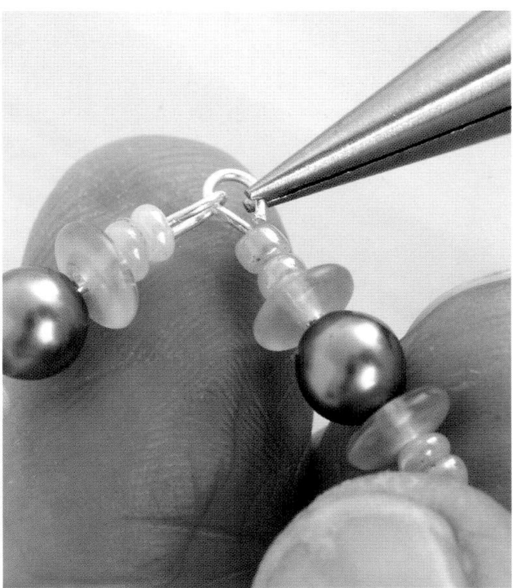

1 When opening a loop, hold the headpin or link firmly in one hand and grasp the side of the loop with snipe-nosed pliers. Push down or up to open the loop. Never pull the ring open as this distorts the nice round shape.

2 Hook on the bead link or finding and close the loop by reversing the action. Make sure that any gaps are closed so that the links don't come apart.

3 Use two pairs of pliers to open a jump ring. If you only have one pair of snipe-nosed or flat-nosed pliers use the round-nosed pliers as well. Close the jump ring using two pairs of pliers as well.

Templates

THIS SECTION CONTAINS THE TEMPLATES YOU WILL NEED FOR SOME OF THE PROJECTS. THEY HAVE BEEN PRODUCED ACTUAL SIZE (EXCEPT THE STOCKING BELOW) SO ALL YOU NEED TO DO IS TRACE THEM.

STAR STOCKING (PAGE 56)

ENLARGE ON A PHOTOCOPIER BY 200%

SWEET TREAT GARLAND (PAGE 34)

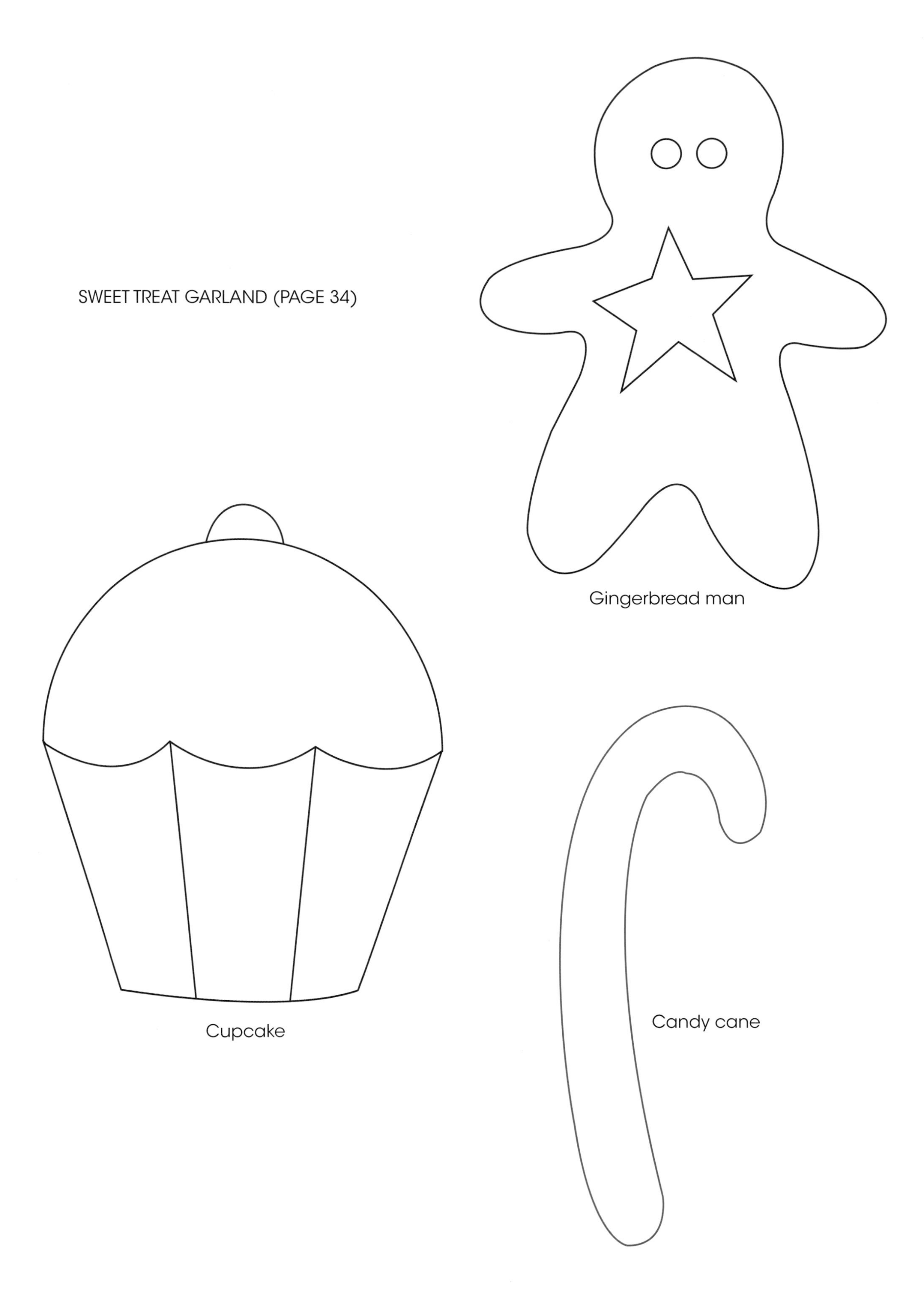

ADVENT GARLAND (PAGE 32)

2 3

1 7

Mitten

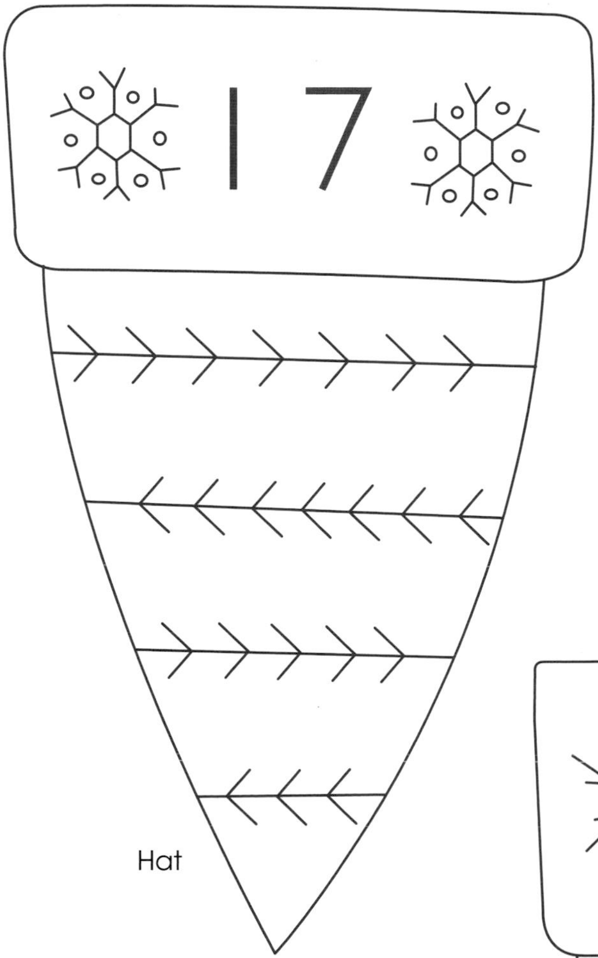

Hat

3

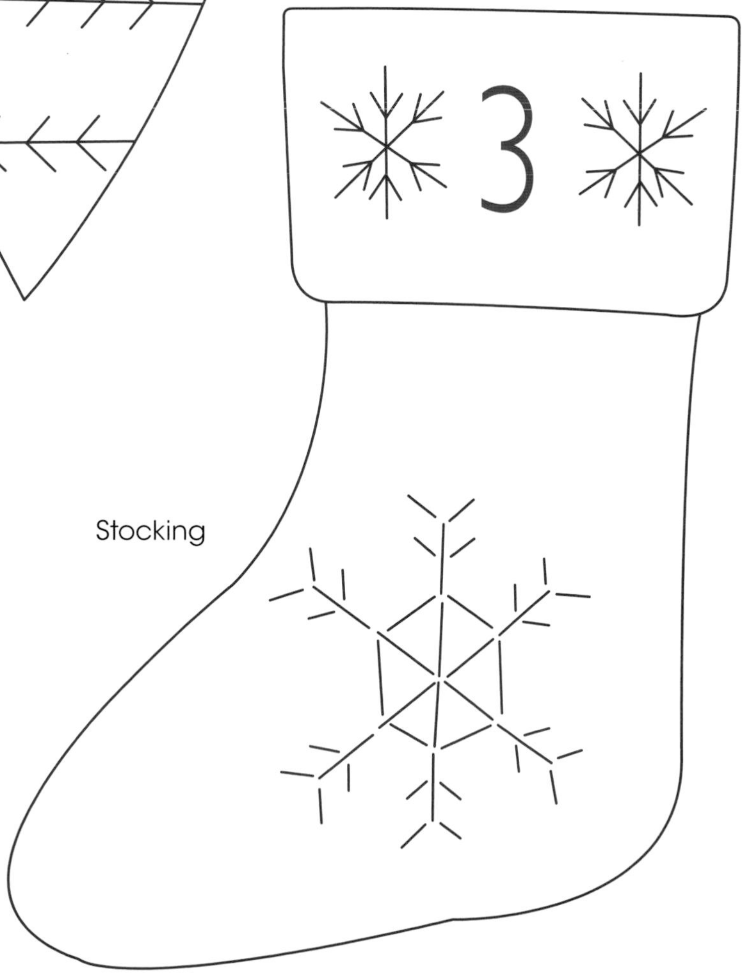

Stocking

4 8
5 9
6 0

RED AND WHITE POINSETTIAS

(PAGES 62 AND 63)

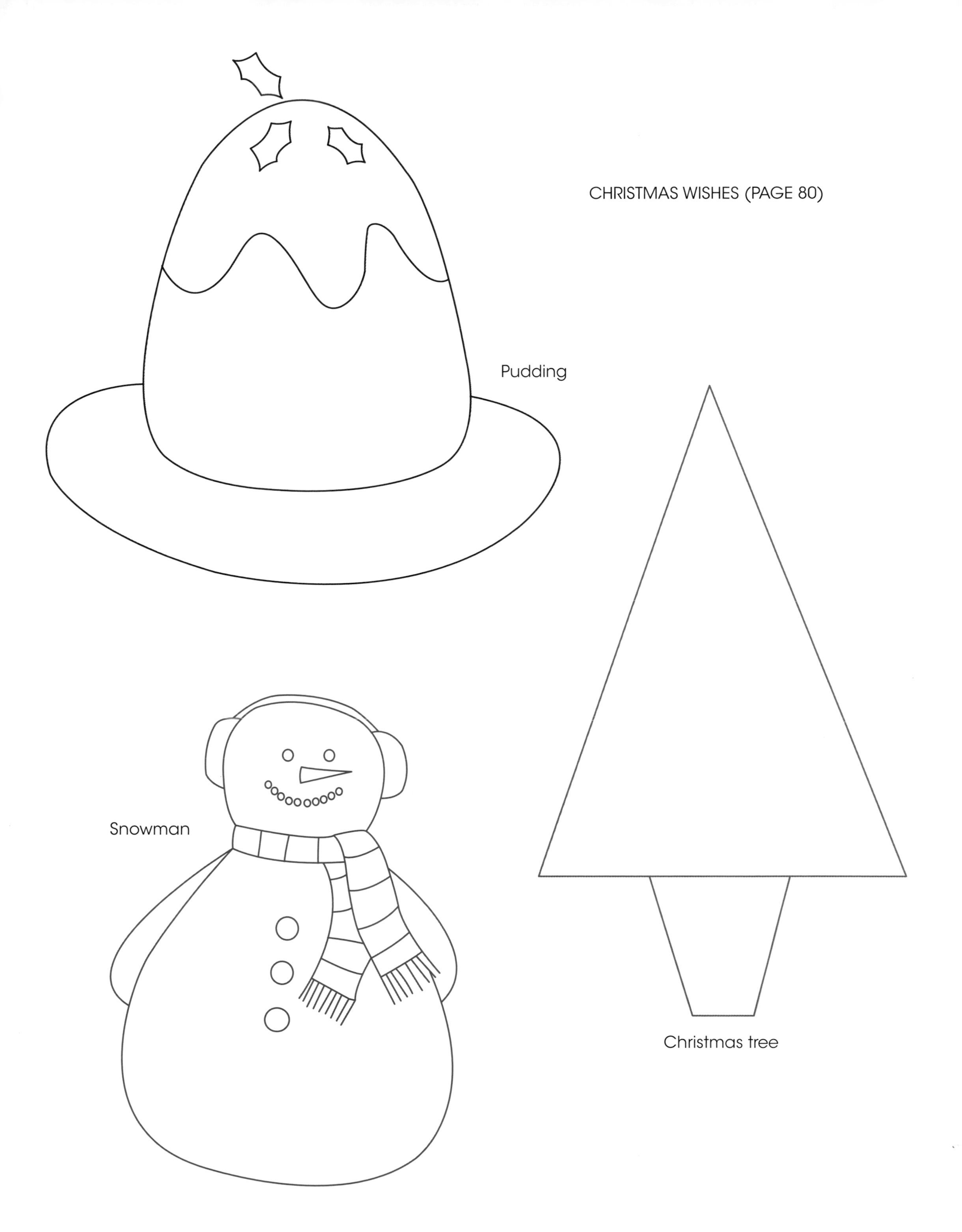
CHRISTMAS WISHES (PAGE 80)
Pudding
Snowman
Christmas tree

Bead project details

THIS LIST CONTAINS DETAILS OF THE VARIOUS BEADS USED IN THE PROJECTS, GIVING COLOURS AND CODES. HOWEVER, THE AVAILABILITY OF BEADS CAN CHANGE SO THE SUPPLIERS LISTED ON PAGE 110 WILL HELP YOU TO SOURCE A VAST VARIETY OF BEADS AND ACCESSORIES.

BEADED SNOWFLAKES (page 16)
Rayher – pearls 6mm (14 401), 8mm (14 402), 10mm (14 403) in white (102), pale blue (356) and silver grey (561); crystals 6mm (14 192), 8mm (14 193), 10mm (14 194) in rock crystal (801), aquamarine (825); grooved metal beads 8mm (16 043), 10mm (16 044) in silver (22); filigree caps 7mm (21 024) and 10mm (21 228) in silver (22).
Local craft shop – silver-lined seed beads size 9 (2.5mm) in clear, blue and grey.
The Bead Shop – snowflake form.

ICICLE DROPLETS (page 17) – as above.

HEX TEALIGHTS (page 20)
Knorr Prandell – seed beads size 9 (2.5mm) silver-lined and size 11 (2mm); satin hex beads in orchid (lilac), orange and mint.
Rayher – bicone crystals 6mm in lilac and fuchsia.

BEADED BLOSSOMS (page 26)
Gütermann – short bugles (603031) white (1016); seed beads size 9 (2.5mm) (773875) dark green (8535); 7mm bugles (773859) dark green (8535); seed beads size 9 (2.5mm) (773875) yellow (1557).
Scientific Wire – dark green and white wire 0.4mm (27swg).

CHRISTMAS KISSES (page 29)
Gütermann – seed beads size 9 (2.5mm) (773875) in silver-lined green (8290).
Rayher – pearls 6mm (14 401) and 8mm (14 402) in white (102).
Kars – 0.45mm (26swg) dark green wire.

ADVENT GARLAND (page 32)
Kars – seed beads size 11 (2mm) in white opaque.
Local craft shop – large white beads, felt and gold bells.

SWEET TREAT GARLAND (page 34)
Gütermann – short bugles (603031) in various pastel shades.
Local craft shop – felt, seed beads, 7mm bugles and sequins.

CHAINLINK CANDLE DROPLETS (page 38)
Gütermann – 10mm facetted drop (614432); 14mm lantern beads (614467) white (1016); diamond-cut 8mm (616451), 10mm (616460); 12 x 21mm drop beads (616478) clear (1016); 10mm ice beads (784192) silver (9495).
Local craft shop – assorted metal ring beads.

SEQUINNED CANDLE (page 39)
Streamers – flat sequins 6mm, 10mm and 16mm in orange, anemone, green, blue and red.
Local craft shop – gold seed beads.

GARLAND CENTREPIECE (page 42)
Gütermann – pearls in 4mm (773883), 6mm (773891) and 8mm (773905) in assorted colours, pale green (7450), pink (5655), deep pink (4805), dark green (8320).
The Spellbound Bead Company – translucent leaf-shaped beads 12 x 7mm.
Scientific wire – 0.5mm (25swg) green wire (3114).

BEADED NAPKIN RING (page 43) – as above.

BEAD TWIST DECORATION (page 46)
The Spellbound Bead Company – Delica beads in white gold (032), galvanized turquoise (415), galvanized satin-finish dark aqua (1183), lined aqua mist AB (078), light aqua pearl (239), satin shimmering white AB, matte white (351).

PEARL SPIRALS (page 47)
Rayher – wax pearls 4mm (16 038), 6mm (16 039) and 10mm (16 004) in silver (22), light blue (08), turquoise (07) and light green (11); tulip-end caps (21 121) in silver (21).
Gütermann – 3-hole bridge in silver (677388).

POMPOM LIGHTS (page 50)
Gütermann – frosted beads 8mm (603066) and 10mm (603074) in yellow (8580), orange (3570), pink (5300), green (8320) and blue (7230).
Knorr Prandell – seed beads size 9 (2.5mm) silver-lined in assorted colours (6203 990); mini light garland (8275 980).

STAR STOCKING (page 56)
Rayher – bicone (polished beads) 5mm (14 212) in rock crystal (801); ball beads (16 300) in silver (22).
Gütermann – seed beads size 9 (2.5mm) (773875) silver-lined clear (1005).

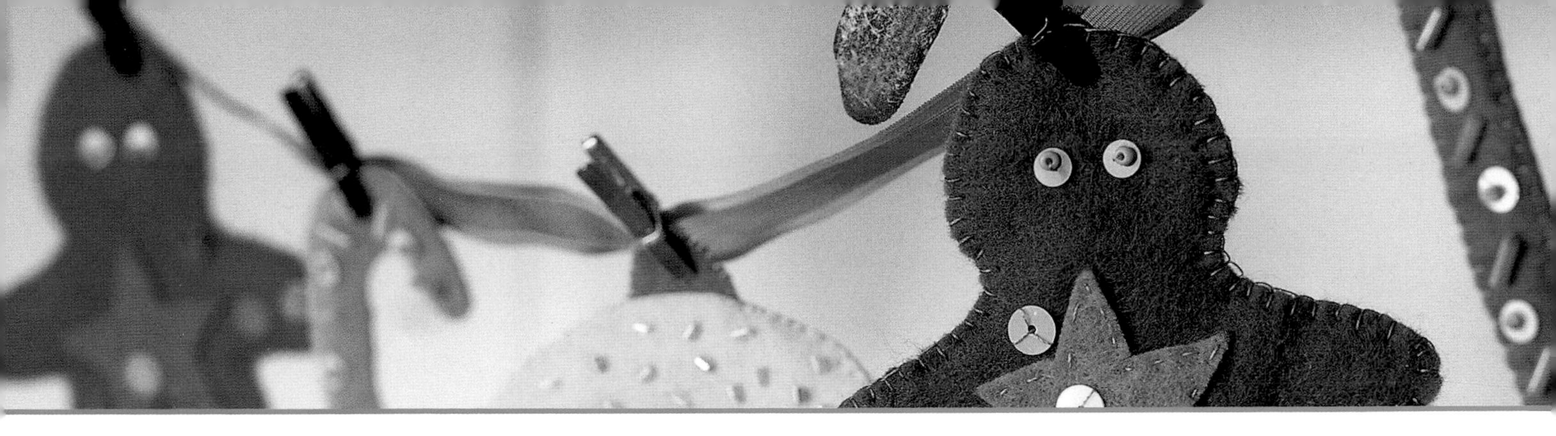

Fibrecrafts – silk viscose velvet, Fibre Etch™.

PIXIE STOCKING (page 58)
Knorr Prandell – ceylon seed beads, mixed pastel (6115 012).
Local craft shop – felt, mixed jewellery and bells.

RED POINSETTIA (page 62)
Gütermann – 3 x 9mm teardrops, 4mm crystals, bugles 20mm, 12mm and 6mm, all in red; 4mm crystals in fuchsia.
Knorr Prandell – seed and pony beads, 3 x 4mm droplets, all in red.
James Hare Silks – silk dupion and organza, red and white.
Local craft shop – net, red and white.

WHITE POINSETTIA (page 63)
Gütermann – 3 x 9mm teardrops; 4mm AB crystals; white 12mm bugles.
Knorr Prandell – silver-lined clear seed beads; white pony beads; 3 x 4mm clear droplets.
James Hare Silks – silk dupion and organza in white.
Local craft shop – net in white.

STAR CARD (page 66)
Efco – sisal shapes, star (34 918 28), snowflake (34 930 07).
Local craft shop – star-shaped beads, red pink and clear; seed beads size 11 (2mm) in red; silver-plated wire 0.4mm (27swg).

RIBBON GIFT BAG (page 70)
Gutermann – teardrops 3 x 9mm (603031) green (8430); 4mm pearls (773883) pink (4805); short bugles (603031) pink (4805); flat oval beads (603007) white (1016); 5mm crystals (601632) green (8430).
Viking Loom – mixed seed bead packs, pale green (HOHO9), pink (HOHO4) and snow and ice (HOHO3).

BEADED BOW NECKLACE (page 74)
Gütermann – multicolour pebbles 15mm (616 494) colour (3665); gold-plated chain with 5mm links.
Viking Loom – bead mix, metallic (BMB 16).

RIBBON CHAIN BRACELET
(page 77) – as above.

CHRISTMAS WISHES CARDS
(page 80)
Knorr Prandell – bead assortments red (8210 020), green (8210 012) and gold (8210 004); 1mm glass beads gold (8206 767) red (8206 155) and green (8206 449); Tacky tape™ film (7901 400).

PRESENT CHARM (page 84)
Bangles and Tat – mix of purple/silver-lined, pink and clear crystal beads in the following types: large decorative beads 10–20mm, tubular beads 5 x 20mm, round crystals 5mm–1cm, smaller decorative beads 5mm–1cm, mixed seed beads 2–4mm, pendant or droplet beads 15–20mm long, large leaf-shaped bead 20 x 35mm, flower bead charms 7 x 10mm, silver beads 2mm.

STAR AND HEART CRACKERS
(pages 88 and 90)
Kars – Swarovski AB crystals, 5mm bicone, 6mm bicone, 6mm flower, 15 x 6mm bicone, Swarovski 12 x 5mm amethyst drop crystal; seed beads size 10 (2.2mm) colour-lined (117 204) purple (5214).
Gütermann – seed beads size 9 (2.5mm) (773875) silver-lined crystal (1005).

FAIRY AND ROBIN CRACKERS
(pages 91 and 92)
Hobbycraft – Mill Hill beads – antique glass beads red (03048), brown (03038), copper (03039), cream (00123); 8mm bugles brown (72023 and 82023) and cream (80123).

Suppliers

UK AND EUROPE

Bangles and Tat
3 Pass Courtyard, off Market St, Ashby de la Zouch, Leicestershire LE65 1AG
tel: 01530 560930
email:
banglesandtat@btinternet.com
www. banglesandtat.co.uk

Efco Hobby Products
Sinotex UK Ltd, Unit D The Courtyard Business Centre, Dover's Farm, Lonesome Lane, Reigate, Surrey RH2 7QT
tel: 01737 245450
email: info@sinotex.co.uk
www.sinotex.co.uk

Fibrecrafts
Old Portsmouth Road, Peasmarsh, Guildford, Surrey GU3 1LZ
tel: 01483 565800
email: sales@fibrecrafts.com
www.fibrecrafts.com

Gütermann and Knorr Prandell
Perivale-Gütermann Ltd, Bullsbrook Road, Hayes, Middlesex UB4 OJR
Gütermann tel: 0208 589 1600
Knorr Prandell tel: 0208 589 1624
email: perivale@guetermann.com
www. guetermann.com

Hobbycraft
For nearest store tel: 0800 027 2387
Mail order: The Peel Centre, St Ann Way, Gloucester, Gloucestershire, GL1 5SF
tel: 0845 051 6522
www.hobbycraft.co.uk

James Hare Silks
PO Box 72, Monarch House, Queen Street, Leeds LS1 1LX
tel: 0113 243 1204
email: sales@jameshares ilks.co.uk
www.jameshar esilks.co.uk

Kars (UK Office)
PO Box 272, Aylesbury, Buckinghamshire HP18 9FH
tel: 01844-238080
email: info@kars.nl
www.kars.biz

Rayher Hobby
Fockestrasse 15, 88471 Laupeim, Germany
tel: 07392 7005 0
email: info@rayher-hobby.de
www.rayher-hobby.de

The Scientific Wire Company
18 Raven Road, South Woodford, London E18 1HW
tel: 020 8505 0002
fax: 020 8559 1114
www.wires.co.uk

Streamers
Unit 1 Tavistock House, Tavistock Street, Bletchley, Milton Keynes MK2 2PG
tel: 01908 644411
email: sales@streamers.co.uk
www.streamers.co.uk

The Bead Shop
7 Market Street, Nottingham NG1 6HY
tel: 0115 958 8899
email: info@mailorder-beads.co.uk
www.mailorder-beads.co.uk

The Spellbound Bead Company
45 Tamworth Street, Lichfield, Staffordshire WS13 6JW
tel: 01543 417650
email: info@spellboundbead.co.uk
www.spellboundbead.co.uk

The Viking Loom
22 High Petergate, York YO1 7EH
tel: 01904 765599
email: vikingloom@vikingloom.co.uk
www.vikingloom.co.uk

USA

Beadie's Beadwork
19985 Westover Avenue, Rocky River, OH 44116
tel: 440 263 5283
email:
beadies@beadiesbeadwork.com
www.beadiesbeadwork.com

Beadworks
149 Water Street, Norwalk, CT 06854
tel: 203 852 9108
email: beads@beadworks.com
www.beadworks.com

Gütermann of America Inc
8227 Arrowbridge Boulevard, PO Box 7387, Charlotte, NC 28241-7387
tel: 704 525 7068
www. guetermann.com

Mill Hill, a division of Wichelt Imports Inc
N162 Hwy 35, Stoddard WI 54658
tel: 608 788 4600
fax: 608 788 6040
email: millhill@millhill.com
www.millhill.com

ACKNOWLEDGMENTS

Many thanks to the following companies for so generously supplying beads and materials for this book: Efco, Perivale-Gütermann, Knorr Prandell, Kars and Rayher Hobby. Thanks to the editorial and design teams at David & Charles, who have done such a wonderful job putting the book together and to Simon Whitmore for the gorgeous photographs. Thanks also to Ali Sharland, who let us take over her lovely home near Stroud for a few days for the finished photography. Finally, thanks to my niece, Kirsty Fraser, a textile student who designed the sweet treat garland and helped make up some of the projects.

ABOUT THE AUTHOR

Dorothy Wood is a talented and prolific craft maker and author. Since completing a course in Advanced Embroidery and Textiles at Goldsmith's College, London, she has written over 20 craft books on all kinds of subjects, and this is her seventh for David & Charles. Dorothy also contributes to several well-known craft magazines, including *Crafts Beautiful* and *Beautiful Cards*. Dorothy lives in the small village of Osgathorpe, Leicestershire, UK.

Index